THE NEW GARDEN SURVIVAL BIBLE

5 IN 1

The Definitive Guide to Design and Build
Your Ultimate Homestead & Prepper's Greenhouse
to Grow, Harvest and Store Your Own Food
for Self-Sufficiency

Jackson P. Howard

TABLE OF CONTENTS

INTRODUCTION TO SURVIVAL GARDENING   10

CHAPTER 1: WELCOME TO SURVIVAL GARDENING   11
The Importance of Self-sufficiency   13
Overview of the Book   15

CHAPTER 2: UNDERSTANDING SURVIVAL GARDENING   16
What is a Survival Garden?   18
Benefits of Growing Your Own Food   20
Quality of Produce   20
Financial Savings   21
Environmental Benefits   21
Physical and Mental Health Benefits   21
Learning Experience and Skill Development   22
Creativity and Personal Expression   22
Supporting Local Communities   22
Key Principles of Survival Gardening   22

PART 1: PREPARING YOUR GARDEN   25

CHAPTER 3: PLANNING YOUR SURVIVAL GARDEN   26
Assessing Your Space and Resources   27
Climate Considerations   29
Designing Your Garden Layout   30

CHAPTER 4: SOIL PREPARATION   35
Understanding Soil Types   36
Soil Testing and Amendment   42
Testing Soil   42
Amending Soil   43
Ongoing Soil Management   45
Composting for Healthy Soil   45
How to Compost   46

CHAPTER 5: WATER MANAGEMENT   **48**

Efficient Irrigation Techniques   **50**

Rainwater Harvesting   **56**

Why Rainwater Harvesting is Important   56

When Rainwater Harvesting Becomes Necessary   56

How to Implement Rainwater Harvesting   57

Managing Water Resources in Drought   **58**

Understanding Water Needs and Prioritization   58

Drought-Resistant Plants and Landscaping   60

CHAPTER 6: BUILDING GARDEN STRUCTURES   **61**

Raised Beds and Container Gardening   **62**

Raised Beds: An Overview   62

Container Gardening: An Overview   63

Comparing Raised Beds and Container Gardening   64

Trellises and Supports   **65**

Greenhouses and Cold Frames   **68**

PART 2: GROWING YOUR CROPS   **70**

CHAPTER 7: CHOOSING THE RIGHT PLANTS   **71**

Essential Survival Crops   **71**

Companion Planting   **74**

Crop Rotation and Polycultures   **75**

Crop Rotation   75

Polyculture   77

CHAPTER 8: STARTING FROM SEED   **80**

Seed Selection and Storage   **81**

Seed Starting Techniques   **82**

Transplanting Seedlings   **84**

CHAPTER 9: VEGETABLE GARDENING   **86**

Root Vegetables: Carrots, Beets, Potatoes   **87**

Carrots   88

Beets   88

Potatoes   88

Leafy Greens: Spinach, Kale, Lettuce   **89**

Spinach   89

Kale   90

Lettuce   90

Fruiting Vegetables: Tomatoes, Peppers, Squash   **91**

Tomatoes   91

Peppers   92

Squash   92

CHAPTER 10: FRUIT AND NUT TREES   **94**

Selecting and Planting Fruit Trees   **94**

Choosing the Right Fruit Trees   94

Preparing for Planting   95

Planting Fruit Trees   95

Caring for Young Fruit Trees   96

Pest and Disease Management   96
Harvesting and Enjoying Your Fruit   96
Nut Trees for Long-Term Sustainability   **97**
Choosing Nut Trees   97
Preparing for Planting   98
Planting Nut Trees   98
Caring for Nut Trees   99
Pest and Disease Management   99
Harvesting and Storing Nuts   99
Long-Term Sustainability and Benefits   100
Berry Bushes and Vines   **100**
Choosing Berry Bushes and Vines   100
Preparing for Planting   101
Planting Berry Bushes and Vines   101
Caring for Berry Bushes and Vines   102
Pest and Disease Management   102
Harvesting and Enjoying Your Berries   103
Long-Term Sustainability and Benefits   103

CHAPTER 11: HERBS AND MEDICINAL PLANTS   **104**
Culinary Herbs: Basil, Mint, Rosemary   **104**
Basil: The Versatile Herb   105
Mint: The Hardy Herb   106
Rosemary: The Aromatic Evergreen   107
Integrating Herbs into Your Garden   107
Medicinal Herbs and Their Uses   **108**
Echinacea   108
Lavender   109
Peppermint   110
Chamomile   110
Calendula   111
Thyme   112
Harvesting and Using Medicinal Herbs   112
Long-Term Sustainability and Benefits   113
Growing and Harvesting Herbs   **113**

PART 3: GARDEN MAINTENANCE AND PROBLEM-SOLVING   **115**

CHAPTER 12: PEST AND DISEASE MANAGEMENT   **116**
Identifying Common Pests and Diseases   **116**
Organic Pest Control Methods   **122**
Disease Prevention and Treatment   **126**

CHAPTER 13: GARDEN CARE AND MAINTENANCE   **130**
Mulching and Weed Control   **130**
Understanding Mulching: What It Is and Why It Matters   131
Types of Mulch and Their Specific Benefits   132

Weed Control: Strategies for Keeping Your Garden Weed-Free   134

Pruning and Training Plants   **135**

Understanding Pruning: Why It's Important   135

Training Plants: Shaping for Success   136

Practical Tips for Pruning and Training   137

Seasonal Garden Tasks   **138**

Spring   138

Summer   138

Fall   138

Winter   139

CHAPTER 14: MAXIMIZING YIELD IN SMALL SPACES   **140**

Vertical Gardening Techniques   **140**

Trellises   141

Arbors and Pergolas   141

Vertical Planters   142

Green Walls   142

Espalier   143

Hanging Gardens   143

Wall Mounts   144

Vertical Hydroponics   144

Intensive Planting Methods   **145**

Square Foot Gardening   145

Companion Planting   145

Interplanting   145

Vertical Gardening   146

Raised Bed Gardening   146

Succession Planting   146

Intensive Row Planting   146

Multi-Layered Planting   147

Intercropping for High Yields   **147**

PART 4: HARVESTING AND PRESERVATION   **149**

CHAPTER 15: HARVESTING TECHNIQUES   **150**

When and How to Harvest   **151**

Timing Your Harvest   152

Fruiting Vegetables   152

Root and Bulb Vegetables   152

Harvesting for Preservation   152

General Best Practices   153

Post-Harvest Handling and Storage   153

Proper Harvesting Tools   **153**

Storing Fresh Produce   **156**

1. Understanding Storage Needs   156

2. Best Practices for Storage   156

3. Specific Storage Techniques for Common Produce   157

CHAPTER 16: FOOD PRESERVATION METHODS   158
    Canning and Bottling   158
    Drying and Dehydrating   162
    Freezing and Fermentation   166
    Freezing   166
    Fermentation   167

CHAPTER 17: SAVING SEEDS FOR THE FUTURE   170
    Seed Saving Techniques   170
    Storing and Preserving Seeds   172
    Planning for Next Season   173

PART 5: SUSTAINABLE PRACTICES AND ADVANCED TECHNIQUES   176

CHAPTER 18: PERMACULTURE PRINCIPLES   177
    Introduction to Permaculture   177
    Designing a Permaculture Garden   178
    Integrating Animals into the Garden   182

CHAPTER 19: ADVANCED GARDENING TECHNIQUES   185
    Hydroponics and Aquaponics   186
    Urban and Rooftop Gardening   188
    Innovative Garden Technologies   190

CHAPTER 20: CREATING A RESILIENT HOMESTEAD   193
    Long-Term Food Storage   193
    Energy and Resource Management   196
    Building Community Resilience   197

GLOSSARY OF GARDENING TERMS   199
    Common Terms and Definitions   199

INDEX OF PLANTS AND TECHNIQUES   203

CONCLUSION   106

INTRODUCTION TO SURVIVAL GARDENING

CHAPTER 1

WELCOME TO SURVIVAL GARDENING

First off, let me just say how awesome it is that you're interested in survival gardening. It's a hobby that's as rewarding as it is practical, it isn't just about planting seeds and hoping for the best—it's about creating a self-sustaining source of food that can see you through tough times, give you peace of mind, and even bring a lot of joy and satisfaction in the process.

Now, you might be wondering, "What exactly is survival gardening, and why is it something I should be thinking about?" Great question! Survival gardening is about growing your own food in a way that ensures you and your family have a reliable, sustainable supply of fresh produce no matter what's going on in the world. It's about being prepared, sure, but it's also about taking control of your own food security and learning some pretty invaluable skills along the way.

Getting started doesn't have to be overwhelming. Maybe you've got a big backyard, a small balcony, or just a windowsill—there are many ways to adapt survival gardening to fit your space and your lifestyle. We'll talk about everything from choosing the right crops to making the most of your resources (like water and soil), and even how to preserve your harvest so you've got food to last through any situation.

One of the best things about survival gardening is how empowering it can be. There's something incredibly satisfying about knowing that you can provide for yourself and your loved ones, no matter what. Plus, it's a skill that only gets better with time. The more you dig in—literally—the more you'll learn about what works best for you, your climate, and your space. And don't worry, you don't need to be a seasoned gardener to get started.

Another thing to keep in mind is that survival gardening is not a hobby; it's a mindset. It's about thinking ahead, being resourceful, and making the most of what you have; it's about community—learning from others, sharing tips, and maybe even trading seeds or produce with your neighbors. And if you're into the idea of living more sustainably or reducing your carbon footprint, survival gardening ticks those boxes, too. We'll cover each of these aspects in detail as we go along.

And here's the real kicker—survival gardening is fun. Seriously. There's something so deeply satisfying about watching those first sprouts poke through the soil, or harvesting your first batch of homegrown vegetables. It's a way to connect with nature, to slow down and appreciate the simple things, and to get down in the dirt in the best possible way. Plus, you get to eat the results of your hard work, which is always a win in our book.

We're going to cover everything you need to know to get started with survival gardening, from the basics to some more advanced tips and tricks. When you're done, you'll have the skills and confidence to turn whatever space you've got into a productive, thriving garden that can keep you and your family fed through good times and bad.

THE IMPORTANCE OF SELF-SUFFICIENCY

Self-sufficiency is one of those concepts that carries a lot of weight, especially when we're talking about something as essential as survival gardening. It's a fundamental principle that underpins the entire idea of growing your own food, particularly in uncertain times. Why is self-sufficiency so important, especially in the context of survival gardening, and what does it really mean for you and your gardening plans? Let's lay the groundwork.

First off, self-sufficiency is about freedom and independence. In today's world, we're all pretty dependent on a complex network of systems to get our food. From the farms where it's grown, to the factories where it's processed, to the trucks that transport it, and finally to the grocery store where you pick it up—there's a long chain of events that have to go just right for you to have that loaf of bread or those fresh vegetables on your plate. But what happens when there's a disruption in that chain? Maybe it's a natural disaster, economic instability, or even something like a pandemic that throws a wrench into the system. Suddenly, the food you've always taken for granted isn't as easy to come by. That's where self-sufficiency comes in; you're no longer at the mercy of supply chains, grocery store shelves, or even the weather to a certain extent because you've taken control of your food production. You've got the freedom to decide what you grow, how you grow it, and how much you store away for the future.

Beyond just the practical aspects, there's a huge psychological benefit to self-sufficiency. Knowing that you can provide for yourself and your loved ones, no matter what happens, is incredibly empowering. It brings a sense of security that money can't buy. When you're self-sufficient, you're less worried about the "what ifs" of the world because you know you've got a plan, and more importantly, the ability to execute that plan. It's like having an insurance policy that's not just a piece of paper but a living, breathing part of your daily life. Every time you plant a seed, harvest a crop, or preserve food for the winter, you're reinforcing that safety net.

There's also a financial aspect to consider. The cost of food has been steadily rising, and depending on where you live, certain fresh produce can be quite expensive, especially if you're trying to eat healthily. Think about it: the cost of a packet of seeds is minimal compared to the amount of food those seeds can produce. Over time, the savings add up, especially if you're able to produce enough to can or freeze and store for the long term. And, if you get really good at it, you might even have a surplus that you can sell or trade with others, adding a little extra income or barter power into the mix.

Another aspect of self-sufficiency is the quality of food you're able to produce. When you're in control of your own food supply, you're not just growing any food—you're growing the best quality food you can. You're in charge of what goes into your soil, what kind of seeds you use, and whether or not you use any pesticides or chemicals.

This means you can grow organic produce if that's important to you. The nutritional value of homegrown food is often higher than store-bought options because you can pick it at peak ripeness and consume it fresh. Plus, there's the taste factor—homegrown just tastes better, doesn't it? There's something about a tomato that ripened in your garden that's worlds apart from one that was picked green and ripened in a warehouse somewhere.

Self-sufficiency also ties deeply into sustainability. In a world that's increasingly aware of the environmental impact of our actions, growing your own food is one of the most direct ways you can reduce your carbon footprint. Think about all the resources that go into bringing food to your table: the fuel for transportation, the energy used in processing, the packaging materials, and so on. When you grow your own food, all of that is minimized. You're also more likely to practice sustainable gardening techniques, like composting, rainwater harvesting, and crop rotation, all of which contribute to the health of your local ecosystem. You're not just providing for yourself; you're doing it in a way that's kind to the planet.

But it's not all serious business—self-sufficiency in gardening can also be a lot of fun. It's a **creative and fulfilling** endeavor that allows you to experiment with different plants, garden layouts, and growing techniques. There's a real joy in the process, from planning your garden to the daily care of your plants, to the satisfaction of the harvest. It's good for your body, mind, and soul. And it's something that can be shared—whether it's getting your kids involved, teaching friends and neighbors, or participating in community gardening projects. Self-sufficiency doesn't have to mean going it alone; it can be a way to connect with others and build a stronger, more resilient community.

Speaking of community, self-sufficiency has a **social aspect**, as well. When more people in a community are self-sufficient, the entire community becomes more resilient. If everyone on your block has a garden, and there's a food shortage or a disaster, suddenly there's a network of people who can help each other out. You might grow more tomatoes than you can eat, while your neighbor has an abundance of cucumbers. Trading and sharing resources like this builds bonds between people and strengthens the fabric of the community. In a broader sense, it creates a culture of preparedness and mutual support that benefits everyone involved.

Finally, there's the tremendous **personal growth** interwoven in the process. Self-sufficiency through gardening is a continuous learning process. It challenges you to acquire new skills, solve problems, and adapt to changing circumstances. Whether it's figuring out why your lettuce isn't growing as well as it should, learning how to deal with pests organically, or mastering the art of canning and preserving, there's always something new to learn. This not only keeps your mind sharp but also builds a sense of accomplishment and confidence. The skills you gain through self-sufficient gardening are transferable to other areas of life, making you a more capable and resourceful person overall.

Ultimately, survival gardening paves the way for self-sufficiency, which gives you freedom, security, and control over your food supply.

OVERVIEW OF THE BOOK

This book on survival gardening will introduce you into the world of self-sufficient living through the art of growing your own food, specifically created for those who want to be prepared for anything life might throw at them. Throughout this journey, you will be developing resilience, independence, and peace of mind in a world where the future can be uncertain.

We will explore survival gardening as a practical, hands-on approach to ensuring that you and your loved ones have a reliable, sustainable source of food no matter what challenges arise. It will walk you through the essentials of creating a garden that can thrive even in less-than-ideal conditions, covering topics like choosing the right crops, maximizing small spaces, and preserving food for long-term storage.

We will also focus on the importance of self-sufficiency—not just as a way to save money or eat healthier, but as a critical strategy for maintaining control over your food supply in times of crisis. It will highlight how survival gardening enables you to take charge of your well-being, offering the freedom to grow what you need and the skills to do so successfully.

This book will also look into the psychological and emotional benefits of survival gardening. You will learn how this practice can enhance your sense of security, reduce your reliance on external systems, and build a deeper connection with the natural world.

Throughout the book, sustainability, self-sufficiency, and environmental responsibility are highly emphasized time and again, showing you how you can grow food in a way that's good for the planet as well as for yourselves. Topics like composting, water conservation, and organic gardening are woven in, providing our readers with the knowledge they need to garden in a way that's both effective and eco-friendly.

Finally, the book will explore the broader implications of survival gardening, including its role in fostering community resilience and its potential to reduce food insecurity on a larger scale. Teaching others how to grow their own food and sharing resources within your community contribute to a more sustainable and secure future for everyone.

So, let's get into it.

CHAPTER 2

UNDERSTANDING SURVIVAL GARDENING

Survival gardening plays an instrumental role in creating a reliable source of food that you control, especially in times when external food systems might be unreliable. Imagine this: economic instability, natural disasters, or other unexpected events could disrupt the food supply chain that you typically rely on. Survival gardening offers a way to mitigate those risks by ensuring you have a stable, self-sufficient source of nourishment right in your own backyard—or even on a balcony or windowsill. You get to take charge of your food security and prepare for various scenarios where access to food might become uncertain.

Understanding the importance of self-sufficiency is key to grasping the value of survival gardening. Think about the current food systems: from the farms where produce is grown, to the factories where it's processed, to the trucks that transport it, and finally to the grocery store where you buy it. That's a long chain of events that needs to function perfectly for you to get that fresh tomato or loaf of bread. If any link in this chain breaks—due to a natural disaster, economic trouble, or even a supply chain hiccup—you might find yourself scrambling for food. You have the freedom to decide what you grow, how you grow it, and how much you store for future use.

Well, what about the psychological boost it provides? There's something incredibly empowering about knowing you can provide for yourself and your loved ones, regardless of what's happening in the world. This sense of security is a form of peace that you can't easily get from a supermarket or an emergency supply kit. When you're self-sufficient, you've got a plan, and you're actively working to ensure that plan is successful. Each time you plant a seed, tend to your garden, or harvest your crops, you're reinforcing that sense of control and security.

Now, let's talk about the practical side of things. Survival gardening involves a few key components that you need to understand to get started. First up is crop selection. Not all plants are created equal when it comes to survival gardening. You'll want to choose crops that are easy to grow as well as resilient and capable of being stored for long periods. Think potatoes, beans, and squash—these are hardy, high-yield plants that can provide a lot of food with relatively little effort.

Next is soil health. Healthy soil is the foundation of a successful garden. You'll need to understand how to improve and maintain soil quality through composting, mulching, and perhaps even creating your own compost. Good soil supports strong plant growth and helps produce a better yield.

Water management is another crucial aspect. Depending on your local climate, you might need to implement rainwater harvesting systems or drip irrigation to ensure your plants get the moisture they need without wasting resources. Water is a vital resource, and managing it efficiently can make a big difference in the success of your garden.

Food preservation is also essential. Once you've grown your crops, you'll need to know how to store them for the long haul. Techniques like canning, drying, and freezing will help you keep your produce fresh and edible even when it's not in season. This step is crucial for ensuring you have food available throughout the year.

In addition to these practical tips, let's not overlook the emotional and financial benefits of survival gardening. Growing your own food can save you a considerable amount of money. Seeds are relatively inexpensive compared to buying produce from the store, and a well-maintained garden can yield a significant amount of food. This cost-saving aspect becomes even more apparent over time as you continue to grow and harvest your own crops.

On the emotional side, gardening offers a unique form of therapy. There's a profound satisfaction in watching your plants grow and thrive, knowing that your hard work is paying off. It's a way to connect with nature and take a break from the hustle and bustle of daily life. Plus, the taste of fresh, homegrown produce is often far superior to store-bought alternatives. It's a joy that goes beyond just the practical aspects of food production.

Understanding survival gardening also means recognizing its role in sustainability. Growing your own food reduces your reliance on external resources and minimizes your carbon footprint. You're not contributing to the energy and resource consumption involved in transporting and packaging food from far-off places. Composting, conserving water, and using organic gardening practices helps to preserve the environment and promote a healthier planet.

Accounting for all these factors, we can see how survival gardening becomes a multifaceted practice that combines practical skills with deeper personal and environmental benefits. Grow food that can sustain you in times of uncertainty, gain the independence and peace of mind that come from self-sufficiency, and embrace a lifestyle that's both fulfilling and sustainable—with a bit of planning and a lot of execution, it all becomes a piece of cake.

WHAT IS A SURVIVAL GARDEN?

A survival garden, as opposed to your everyday patch of greens, is a strategic, carefully planned space designed to provide a sustainable and reliable source of food, especially during times of crisis or uncertainty. This type of garden is all about self-sufficiency, making sure you have the essential nutrients you need without relying on grocery stores or external food supplies that might not always be available. It's a lifeline, a safety net that you create with your own hands, and it's as much about peace of mind as it is about producing food.

So, what does a survival garden look like? While the exact appearance can vary depending on your available space, climate, and personal preferences, there are some key elements and characteristics that most survival gardens share.

1. Practical Layout:

A survival garden is typically organized with efficiency and productivity in mind. You won't find sprawling lawns or decorative flower beds here—every inch of space is utilized for growing food. Raised beds, row planting, and companion planting techniques are often employed to maximize the yield from the available area. The garden layout is usually compact and functional, with pathways that allow easy access to all plants for maintenance and harvesting. Some survival gardens might use square foot gardening, where plants are densely planted in small spaces to get the most out of the available soil.

2. Diversity of Crops:

A survival garden is designed to produce a wide variety of crops to meet your nutritional needs. You'll see a mix of root vegetables (like potatoes and carrots), leafy greens (like spinach and kale), legumes (like beans and peas), and fruits (like tomatoes and berries). The idea is to grow a balanced diet that provides essential vitamins, minerals, and calories. This diversity also helps protect against crop failures; if one type of plant doesn't do well one season, you've got plenty of others to rely on.

3. Perennials and Self-Seeding Plants:

Survival gardens often include a good number of perennial plants—those that come back year after year without needing to be replanted. These might include herbs like rosemary and thyme, vegetables like asparagus, and fruits like berry bushes or fruit trees. Perennials are valuable because they require less work and provide a reliable harvest every season. Additionally, survival gardens may include self-seeding annuals, which drop seeds that grow into new plants the following year, further reducing the need for manual planting.

4. Nutrient-Dense Plants:

Because survival gardening is about producing the maximum amount of nutrition from your garden, you'll find that many of the plants chosen are those that are particularly rich in essential nutrients. This includes dark leafy greens like kale and spinach, which are high in vitamins A and C, as well as calorie-dense crops like potatoes, sweet potatoes, and winter squash. Beans and legumes are also staples because they're rich in protein and can help sustain your energy levels.

5. Preservation Focus:

Survival gardens focus on what you can store for the long term. You'll see crops that are easy to preserve, like tomatoes (for canning), beans (which can be dried), and root vegetables like carrots and beets (which can be stored in a root cellar). The layout might include specific spaces for drying herbs, hanging onions and garlic, or setting up canning stations. Preservation is a key component because the goal is to have food available not just in the growing season, but throughout the entire year.

6. Water Conservation Features:

Given that water might be a scarce resource during a crisis, survival gardens often incorporate water conservation techniques. You might see rain barrels collecting water from gutters, drip irrigation systems that minimize water waste, or mulched beds that help retain moisture in the soil. The garden might also be designed with swales or berms that direct rainwater toward the plants that need it most. Efficient water use is crucial in a survival garden because it ensures that your crops can thrive even in drought conditions.

7. Companion Planting and Pest Control:

Survival gardens often make use of companion planting, where certain plants are grown together because they benefit each other in some way. For example, planting marigolds near tomatoes can help deter pests, while beans can fix nitrogen in the soil to help nearby plants grow better. This reduces the need for chemical fertilizers and pesticides, which might not be available during a crisis. You might also see natural pest control methods like traps, barriers, or the introduction of beneficial insects that prey on garden pests.

8. Compact and Vertical Gardening:

If space is limited, a survival garden might incorporate vertical gardening techniques. This includes growing plants up trellises, in stacked containers, or even using wall-mounted planters. Vertical gardening allows you to grow more food in a smaller footprint, making it ideal for urban or suburban settings where yard space might be limited. You might also see the use of hanging baskets for herbs or strawberries, maximizing every available space.

9. Self-Reliance Features:

The design of a survival garden often reflects a mindset of self-reliance. This could mean the inclusion of a composting area to recycle kitchen scraps into valuable soil nutrients or a seed-saving station where you can dry and store seeds for the next planting season. The garden might also include a small greenhouse or cold frame to extend the growing season, allowing you to start plants early in the spring or keep them growing late into the fall.

10. Practical Aesthetics:

While beauty isn't the primary focus, survival gardens can still be attractive. The sight of thriving plants, the smell of fresh herbs, and the vibrant colors of ripening fruits and vegetables create a space that's not only functional but also pleasant to spend time in. However, the aesthetics are usually practical, with function taking precedence. Raised beds, trellises, and even the types of plants chosen often serve multiple purposes—providing food, conserving water, and creating a habitat for beneficial insects.

In essence, a survival garden is a living, growing insurance policy. It's designed with careful consideration of how to make the most of the resources you have, whether that's space, water, or time. It involves creating space to provide sustenance and security and of course having a picture-perfect garden.

BENEFITS OF GROWING YOUR OWN FOOD

Cultivating and growing your own food comes with a number of benefits that extend beyond just having fresh vegetables at your fingertips. From creating a deeper connection with nature to providing financial savings, growing your own food can transform the way you eat, live, and think about the world around you.

QUALITY OF PRODUCE

One of the most obvious benefits of growing your own food is the quality of the produce you get to enjoy. When you harvest vegetables, fruits, or herbs straight from your garden, they are at their peak in terms of flavor and nutritional value. Store-bought produce often travels long distances before it reaches your plate, losing nutrients and flavor along the way. In contrast, homegrown food is fresher, which means it's richer in vitamins, minerals, and antioxidants. You also have complete control over how your food is grown, allowing you to avoid harmful pesticides and chemicals, ensuring that what you eat is as healthy as possible.

FINANCIAL SAVINGS

Growing your own food can significantly reduce your grocery bill. Seeds are inexpensive, and with a little effort, a small garden can produce a substantial amount of food. Over time, the savings can really add up, especially if you focus on high-yield crops like tomatoes, beans, and leafy greens. Moreover, perennial plants like fruit trees or berry bushes can provide food year after year with minimal maintenance, further increasing your return on investment. Even in urban settings, a few pots on a balcony or a small raised bed can provide a steady supply of fresh herbs and vegetables, cutting down on the need to purchase these items at the store.

ENVIRONMENTAL BENEFITS

Cultivating your own food is one of the most environmentally friendly things you can do. Industrial agriculture relies heavily on fossil fuels for planting, harvesting, processing, and transporting food, contributing to greenhouse gas emissions. Home gardens also promote biodiversity, especially when you plant a variety of crops and flowers that attract beneficial insects and pollinators like bees and butterflies. Additionally, by composting kitchen scraps and garden waste, you can create a closed-loop system that recycles nutrients back into the soil, reducing the need for chemical fertilizers and minimizing waste.

PHYSICAL AND MENTAL HEALTH BENEFITS

Gardening is a form of exercise that benefits both the body and mind. The physical activity involved in gardening—digging, planting, weeding, and harvesting—helps build strength, endurance, and flexibility. It's a low-impact activity that's accessible to people of all ages and fitness levels. Beyond the physical benefits, gardening is also known to reduce stress and anxiety. Spending time outdoors, engaging with nature, and focusing on the rhythmic tasks of gardening can have a calming effect, promoting mindfulness and reducing mental fatigue. The act of nurturing plants and watching them grow provides a sense of accomplishment and can be a powerful boost to mental well-being.

LEARNING EXPERIENCE AND SKILL DEVELOPMENT

Gardening is a continuous learning experience that teaches valuable skills. Whether you're learning about soil health, plant biology, pest management, or food preservation, there's always something new to discover. For families, gardening can be an excellent educational tool, teaching children about where their food comes from, the importance of sustainability, and the science behind plant growth. These lessons are hands-on and engaging, making them more impactful than textbook learning. As you develop your gardening skills, you also gain a sense of independence and confidence in your ability to provide for yourself and your family.

CREATIVITY AND PERSONAL EXPRESSION

Gardening allows for a great deal of creativity. From designing the layout of your garden to experimenting with new plant varieties and techniques, there are endless opportunities to express yourself. This creative process can be deeply satisfying, as you see your vision come to life and evolve over time. The satisfaction of harvesting and eating food that you've grown yourself is a unique pleasure that fosters a sense of pride and accomplishment.

SUPPORTING LOCAL COMMUNITIES

In times of surplus, sharing or selling excess produce can support local markets and encourage others in your community to pursue gardening as well. This local focus not only benefits the environment but also strengthens community ties and supports the local economy.

KEY PRINCIPLES OF SURVIVAL GARDENING

The key principles of survival gardening are foundational concepts that guide the creation and maintenance of a garden designed to sustain you during times of need. These principles ensure that your garden is productive, resilient, and capable of providing a continuous supply of food. These principles are listed out below

1 → **Self-Sufficiency:**

The primary goal of survival gardening is to reduce your reliance on external food sources by growing your own. This means selecting crops that provide the most nutrition and can be preserved for long-term storage. You should focus on growing a variety of fruits, vegetables, herbs, and even grains that can meet your dietary needs throughout the year.

2 → Maximizing Yield:

In a survival garden, every square foot of space should be used efficiently to maximize food production. This includes using intensive planting methods like square foot gardening, vertical gardening, and companion planting to increase the amount of food you can grow in a limited area. The idea is to get the most out of your garden with the least amount of space and resources.

3 → Crop Diversity:

Diversity is crucial in survival gardening to ensure a balanced diet and to protect against the risk of crop failures. Planting a variety of crops reduces the chances of losing your entire food supply to pests, diseases, or adverse weather conditions. A diverse garden also ensures that you have a well-rounded diet, with different crops providing essential vitamins, minerals, and calories.

4 → Soil Health:

Healthy soil is the foundation of a productive garden. In survival gardening, maintaining and improving soil fertility is essential. Practices like composting, mulching, crop rotation, and cover cropping help to keep the soil rich in nutrients and capable of supporting high-yield crops. Avoiding chemical fertilizers and pesticides is also important to preserve the long-term health of your soil.

5 → Water Management:

Efficient use of water is a critical principle in survival gardening, especially in areas prone to drought or water shortages. Techniques like mulching, drip irrigation, and rainwater harvesting help to conserve water and ensure that your plants get the moisture they need. Designing your garden to capture and retain water, such as by using swales or berms, can also improve water efficiency.

6 → Perennial and Self-Seeding Plants:

Incorporating perennial plants and self-seeding annuals into your garden reduces the amount of labor required to maintain it and ensures a consistent food supply. Perennials like fruit trees, berry bushes, and asparagus come back year after year, providing food with minimal effort. Self-seeding plants, such as certain herbs and flowers, drop their seeds naturally, which then grow into new plants the following season.

7 → Seed Saving:

To maintain a truly self-sufficient garden, saving seeds from your crops is essential. Seed saving allows you to replant your garden year after year without relying on store-bought seeds. Over time, seeds saved from your garden can also adapt to your specific growing conditions, making your plants more resilient and productive.

8 → Pest and Disease Management:

In a survival garden, you want to minimize the risk of losing crops to pests and diseases. This can be achieved through natural pest control methods, such as attracting beneficial insects, using companion planting to repel harmful pests, and practicing good garden hygiene. Crop rotation and diversity also help to reduce the buildup of pests and diseases in the soil.

9 → Food Preservation:

A key principle of survival gardening is planning for the long term by preserving your harvest. Whether through canning, drying, fermenting, or storing in a root cellar, preserving your produce ensures that you have food available even when your garden isn't producing. This is especially important for survival gardening, where the goal is to create a reliable food source year-round.

10 → Adaptability and Resilience:

A successful survival garden must be adaptable to changing conditions. This means being prepared to adjust your planting schedule, crop selection, and gardening techniques based on the weather, available resources, and any challenges that arise. Building resilience into your garden—such as by growing hardy, drought-resistant crops or setting up a greenhouse—helps ensure that your garden can continue to provide food even in difficult circumstances.

11 → Minimal Reliance on External Inputs:

To achieve true self-sufficiency, a survival garden should minimize dependence on external inputs like fertilizers, pesticides, and even water. Focusing on these sustainable practices reduces the need to rely on outside resources thereby making your garden more resilient.

12 → Community and Knowledge Sharing:

While survival gardening is often focused on individual or family self-sufficiency, it also benefits from a community approach. Sharing knowledge, seeds, and even surplus produce with neighbors can strengthen your local food network and provide mutual support in times of need. Learning from others' experiences and contributing your own insights can help improve the effectiveness and resilience of your survival garden.

That's it for the necessary principles. With an elementary understanding of survival gardens established, we can now start getting into the first steps needed to prepare your garden.

PART 1
PREPARING YOUR GARDEN

CHAPTER 3

PLANNING YOUR SURVIVAL GARDEN

Planning a survival garden involves careful consideration of your needs, available space, and local growing conditions to create a self-sustaining source of food.

Begin by evaluating the space you have available, whether it's a backyard, a balcony, or even indoor areas for container gardening. Consider sunlight exposure, soil quality, and access to water, as these factors will influence what you can grow.

Think about what foods you and your family eat most often and which crops provide the most nutrition. Focus on high-yield, nutrient-dense plants like potatoes, beans, leafy greens, and root vegetables. Also, consider growing perennials like berry bushes and fruit trees for a continuous food supply.

Design your garden with efficiency in mind. Use raised beds, rows, or square foot gardening to maximize space, and incorporate companion planting to improve plant health and reduce pests. If space is limited, think vertically with trellises or stacked planters.

Diversity is key in a survival garden to ensure a balanced diet and resilience against crop failures. Grow a variety of vegetables, herbs, and fruits that can be eaten fresh, stored, or preserved.

Implement water conservation techniques like rain barrels, drip irrigation, and mulching to ensure your garden remains productive even during dry spells.

Include plants that can be preserved for long-term storage, such as tomatoes for canning or beans for drying. Learn seed-saving techniques to maintain your garden year after year without relying on external sources.

If you're new to gardening, start with a manageable size and gradually expand as you gain experience. This allows you to learn what works best in your environment and refine your approach.

ASSESSING YOUR SPACE AND RESOURCES

When it comes to planning a survival garden, the first and most crucial step is assessing your space and resources. This assessment lays the foundation for a garden that's sustainable and capable of supporting you and your family in times of need. Whether you have a sprawling backyard, a modest urban plot, or even just a balcony, understanding the space you have available is essential. Start by measuring the area to get a clear idea of the physical size you're working with.

This measurement will help you determine how much you can realistically grow and what types of plants will fit best in your space. For instance, a larger garden might accommodate a variety of crops, including larger plants like fruit trees or corn, while a smaller space might require a more strategic approach, such as vertical gardening or container planting.

Next, consider the sunlight exposure your space receives. Sunlight is critical for plant growth, and most vegetables need at least six to eight hours of direct sunlight each day to thrive. Take note of areas that get full sun, partial shade, or full shade throughout the day, and plan your garden layout accordingly. If you find that your space has limited sunlight, you might need to focus on crops that can tolerate partial shade, like leafy greens or certain herbs. Additionally, assess the quality of your soil, which is another cornerstone of a successful garden. Healthy, fertile soil is well-draining, rich in organic matter, and balanced in nutrients. Conduct a simple soil test to determine its texture—whether it's sandy, loamy, or clayey—and its pH level. Knowing your soil's characteristics will help you decide what amendments, like compost or organic fertilizers, might be necessary to improve its fertility.

Water access is another vital resource to evaluate. A reliable water source is essential for keeping your garden productive, especially during dry spells. Consider how you'll water your garden—whether you have access to a hose, can collect rainwater, or need to implement water-saving techniques like drip irrigation. In areas where water is scarce, planning for efficient water management is key. This might involve installing rain barrels to capture runoff, using mulch to retain soil moisture, or choosing drought-tolerant plants that require less water to thrive.

As you assess your space, also think about other environmental factors, such as wind patterns and microclimates within your garden. Wind can be damaging to plants, so you might need to create windbreaks with fences, hedges, or taller plants. Similarly, microclimates—areas within your garden where conditions differ slightly, such as a warmer spot near a south-facing wall—can be used to your advantage by planting crops that thrive in those specific conditions.

In addition to physical space and environmental factors, consider the gardening tools and equipment you have available. Having the right tools on hand, such as shovels, hoes, trowels, and watering cans, can make the work of gardening much easier and more efficient. If you're missing essential tools, you may need to invest in them or borrow from a neighbor. Also, think about the seeds and plants you can access. It's wise to focus on heirloom or open-pollinated seeds, which allow you to save seeds from year to year, making your garden more self-sufficient over time.

Another important resource is compost. Composting is an excellent way to recycle kitchen scraps, garden waste, and other organic materials into nutrient-rich soil that can boost your garden's fertility. If you don't already have a compost bin or pile, starting one is a great step toward creating a more sustainable garden. Along with compost, consider other soil amendments you might need, such as manure, bone meal, or lime, depending on your soil's nutrient levels and pH.

Once you've assessed your space and resources, it's important to think about the future. Start with a manageable garden size, but leave room for expansion as you gain experience and confidence. This might mean planning for additional garden beds, fruit trees, or perennial plants that can provide a continuous food source year after year. Flexibility is also key in survival gardening. Be prepared to adapt your plans based on changing conditions, whether those are environmental factors like drought or personal circumstances like a change in your available time or resources. For example, if you notice that water is becoming scarcer, you might switch to more drought-tolerant crops or invest in more efficient irrigation systems.

Finally, don't overlook the value of community resources. Local gardening groups, community gardens, and extension services can provide invaluable support, advice, and even shared resources like seeds and tools. Engaging with your local gardening community can help you troubleshoot challenges and gain new insights into how to make your garden more productive and resilient. This thorough assessment ensures that you make informed decisions about what to grow, how to grow it, and how to manage your garden effectively, setting you on the path to self-sufficiency and food security.

CLIMATE CONSIDERATIONS

When planning and preparing a survival garden, considering the weather and climate is essential to ensure that your efforts are not only fruitful but sustainable in the long run. The climate where you live determines what crops will thrive, how long your growing season is, and the specific challenges your garden might face, such as drought, frost, or extreme heat.

To start, it's crucial to understand your local climate, including your hardiness zone and the length of your growing season. This knowledge helps you choose the right plants that are best suited to your region, whether you're in a temperate zone with a long growing season or a colder area with a shorter window for planting and harvesting.

Once you know your climate, you can begin planning for seasonal changes and potential weather extremes. For example, in spring, late frosts can be a threat to young plants, so it's wise to monitor the weather closely and be prepared with frost protection methods like row covers or cloches. Summer brings its own challenges, especially in regions with high temperatures where heat stress can affect both plants and soil moisture levels. In such conditions, mulching, providing shade, and selecting heat-tolerant crops become vital strategies to maintain a productive garden. Similarly, understanding the first frost dates in fall allows you to plan your harvests and protect late-season crops, while winter gardening in milder climates can keep your garden productive year-round with the right crops and protection measures.

Beyond seasonal planning, preparing for extreme weather conditions is also crucial. Droughts, for instance, require you to adopt water conservation techniques such as drip irrigation, mulching, and choosing drought-tolerant plants to ensure your garden survives prolonged dry periods. On the flip side, excessive rainfall and flooding necessitate good drainage practices, like raised beds, to protect plants from waterlogging. Wind protection is another important consideration, especially in areas prone to strong winds, which can damage plants and dry out the soil. Implementing windbreaks and providing support to vulnerable plants can help mitigate these effects.

As climates are becoming increasingly unpredictable due to global changes, flexibility and adaptability are more important than ever. Microclimates within your garden—like a sunny south-facing wall or a shaded corner—can be used to your advantage by selecting plants that thrive in those specific conditions. Incorporating season extenders such as cold frames, greenhouses, or row covers can help you start your growing season earlier and extend it later, ensuring a longer period of productivity. Lastly, focusing on resilient, adaptable crops, particularly heirloom varieties, can provide a buffer against changing conditions, ensuring that your garden continues to produce even when the weather doesn't cooperate.

DESIGNING YOUR GARDEN LAYOUT

The available space is often a determining factor in how you design and arrange your garden. Whether you have acres of land, a small urban backyard, or just a balcony or windowsill, there are various garden arrangements that can fit your space and still provide you with a sustainable source of food.

Designing these gardens involves creativity and practical planning to maximize productivity, regardless of size or layout constraints. Let's look at different types of survival garden arrangements and how to design them to fit various spaces

1. Traditional Row Gardens

Best for: Large backyards or rural areas with plenty of space.

Design Overview

Traditional row gardens are what most people envision when they think of a garden—a large plot of land where crops are planted in rows. This arrangement is ideal if you have a substantial amount of space and want to grow a variety of crops in larger quantities. Row gardens allow for easy access between plants, making weeding, watering, and harvesting straightforward. They also provide good air circulation, which helps prevent plant diseases.

Design Tips

Orientation: Arrange rows in a north-south orientation to ensure each plant gets maximum sunlight throughout the day.

Spacing: Leave enough space between rows to walk and push a wheelbarrow or garden cart. Typically, 18 to 24 inches between rows is sufficient.

Crop Rotation: Implement crop rotation each season to maintain soil fertility and reduce pest buildup.

Companion Planting: Consider companion planting to maximize space and enhance plant health. For example, plant taller crops like corn alongside shorter ones like beans to create natural shade.

2. Raised Bed Gardens

Best for: Small to medium backyards, urban spaces, or areas with poor soil quality.

Design Overview

Raised bed gardens are a popular choice for small to medium spaces because they allow for more control over soil quality and drainage. Raised beds are essentially large, contained areas filled with soil where plants can be grown closer together than in traditional row gardens. This arrangement is highly productive, easier on the back, and can be designed to fit almost any space.

Design Tips

Size and Shape: Build your raised beds to a size that's easy to work with—typically 3 to 4 feet wide and 6 to 8 feet long, so you can reach the center from either side without stepping on the soil.

Height: Aim for at least 6 to 12 inches in height to provide ample soil depth for roots to grow. Taller beds, around 18 to 24 inches, are great for people with mobility issues and can reduce the need to bend over.

Material: Use durable, non-toxic materials like cedar, stone, or un-treated wood to construct the beds. Avoid treated lumber that may leach chemicals into the soil.

Soil Mix: Fill your beds with a high-quality mix of topsoil, compost, and organic matter to create a rich growing environment. Raised beds warm up faster in the spring, allowing for an earlier start to the growing season.

3. Vertical Gardens

Best for: Small urban spaces, balconies, patios, or areas with limited ground space.

Design Overview

Vertical gardens are ideal for maximizing production in small spaces by growing plants upwards rather than outwards. This type of garden arrangement can be as simple as trellises for climbing plants like cucumbers and beans, or as complex as tiered shelves, wall-mounted planters, or hanging baskets. Vertical gardens make efficient use of space, are visually appealing, and can be a practical solution for urban gardeners.

Design Tips

Choosing Plants: Select plants that naturally climb or trail, such as tomatoes, peas, pole beans, cucumbers, and vining squash. For wall-mounted planters, consider herbs, strawberries, or leafy greens.

Support Structures: Use sturdy materials like metal or wooden trellises, wire frames, or lattice for climbing plants. Ensure that the support structures are securely anchored.

Containers: If using containers, choose ones that are large enough to support root growth and have adequate drainage. Hanging baskets should be lined with moisture-retaining materials like coconut coir.

Watering: Vertical gardens may require more frequent watering due to increased exposure and gravity pulling water down. Consider using drip irrigation or self-watering systems to maintain consistent moisture levels.

4. Container Gardens

Best for: Balconies, patios, rooftops, or indoor spaces with plenty of light.

Design Overview

Container gardens are versatile and can be set up almost anywhere, making them perfect for those with very limited space, such as apartment dwellers or those with only a patio or balcony. Containers can range from traditional pots and planters to repurposed items like buckets or barrels. This method allows you to grow a wide variety of crops, including vegetables, herbs, and small fruit trees.

Design Tips

Container Size: Choose containers that are large enough for the plants you intend to grow while also stable enough to accommodate any support structures like stakes or trellises so that the top is not overburdened. For instance, tomatoes require at least a 5-gallon container to prevent toppling, while smaller pots are sufficient for herbs, which generally don't need additional support.

Soil: Use a high-quality potting mix designed for containers, which is lighter and drains better than garden soil. Adding compost or organic fertilizer will help maintain soil fertility.

Mobility: Consider placing containers on wheeled stands or using lightweight materials so they can be easily moved to chase the sun or avoid bad weather.

Grouping: Group containers with similar water and light needs together to simplify care and create a microclimate that retains humidity.

5. Square Foot Gardens

Best for: Small backyards, urban spaces, or anyone looking for an organized, efficient garden layout.

Design Overview

Square foot gardening is a method that involves dividing a raised bed or garden area into square-foot sections, with each square dedicated to a specific crop. This arrangement is highly efficient, allowing for maximum yield in a small space with minimal waste. It's also an easy system for beginners, as it simplifies planning and planting.

Design Tips

Grid Layout: Create a grid by marking off square feet with string or wood slats. Each square foot is then planted with a specific crop according to its spacing needs (e.g., one tomato plant per square foot, four lettuce plants per square foot).

Crop Rotation: Plan your garden so that different crops occupy each square in successive seasons, which helps maintain soil health and reduces the risk of pests.

Companion Planting: Utilize companion planting principles within the grid to enhance growth and deter pests. For example, plant marigolds or basil alongside tomatoes.

Succession Planting: After harvesting a square, replant it with a new crop to maximize productivity throughout the growing season.

CHAPTER

4

SOIL PREPARATION

Preparing the soil is a fundamental step in establishing a productive survival garden, as it sets the stage for healthy plant growth and optimal yields. The process begins with assessing the soil to understand its current condition. This involves determining the soil's texture—whether it's sandy, loamy, or clayey—as each type affects drainage and nutrient retention differently. Testing the soil's pH is also crucial, as most plants thrive in slightly acidic to neutral conditions (pH 6.0 to 7.0). You can use a soil test kit or consult a local extension office for a detailed analysis.

Once you have a clear understanding of your soil, the next

step is to clear the area of weeds, debris, and existing vegetation. Weeds compete with your plants for resources, so removing them thoroughly is essential. You can pull weeds by hand, use a hoe, or employ smothering techniques like covering the soil with newspaper or cardboard. For larger areas, tilling can help incorporate organic matter and uproot weeds, though it's important to be mindful of potential weed seed dispersal.

Improving soil structure involves adding organic matter to enhance the soil's ability to retain moisture and nutrients. Compost, aged manure, and other organic materials help improve sandy soils' water-holding capacity and loosen clay soils to improve drainage. Mulching after planting helps retain moisture, regulate soil temperature, and suppress weeds. Aerating the soil by tilling or using a garden fork helps alleviate compaction and improves air and water movement, which is particularly important for clay-heavy soils.

Adjusting soil pH if your soil is too acidic, adding lime can help raise the pH, while sulfur or peat moss can lower the pH if the soil is too alkaline. It's important to follow the recommendations from your soil test to avoid over-application, which can negatively impact plant growth.

Enriching the soil with nutrients is certain to ensuring that plants have access to essential elements for growth. Compost and well-rotted manure are excellent organic fertilizers that provide a slow-release source of nutrients. Green manures or cover crops planted in the off-season can add nitrogen and improve soil structure when tilled under. Specific fertilizers may be necessary based on soil test results to address any particular deficiencies.

Preparing the soil for planting involves finalizing the soil structure by leveling and creating beds or mounds if needed. This ensures an even planting surface and facilitates better irrigation. Pre-planting watering helps settle the soil and prepares it for seeds or transplants.

Maintaining soil health is an ongoing process that includes regular mulching to conserve moisture and add organic matter, applying additional fertilizers as needed, practicing crop rotation to prevent nutrient depletion and disease, and continuing composting to enrich the soil.

UNDERSTANDING SOIL TYPES

Understanding your soil type helps you choose the right plants and amendments for successful cultivation. Each soil type has specific needs and challenges, and adapting your gardening practices to match these can significantly improve your garden's productivity and resilience.

SANDY SOIL

Characteristics:

Sandy soil is composed of large particles, which creates a loose, gritty texture. This soil drains quickly and doesn't hold moisture or nutrients well. It warms up rapidly in the spring, which can be advantageous for early planting.

Impact on Survival Gardening:

- Advantages: The quick drainage helps prevent waterlogging and root rot. It's easier to work with and heats up faster, which can extend the growing season.

- Challenges: Sandy soil requires frequent watering and fertilization due to its poor moisture and nutrient retention. Plants may struggle to thrive without additional amendments.

Improvement Strategies:

- Add organic matter such as compost or aged manure to improve moisture and nutrient retention.

- Use mulch to help retain soil moisture and regulate temperature.

CLAY SOIL

Characteristics:

Clay soil is made up of very fine particles that compact tightly together, making it heavy and dense. This soil holds water well but can become waterlogged and slow to drain. It is often cooler and harder to work with when wet.

Impact on Survival Gardening:

• Advantages: Clay soil retains water and nutrients effectively, making it generally fertile.

• Challenges: Poor drainage can lead to waterlogging and root diseases. The soil can become hard and compacted, inhibiting root growth.

Improvement Strategies:

• Add organic matter such as compost or aged manure to improve moisture and nutrient retention.

• Use mulch to help retain soil moisture and regulate temperature.

LOAMY SOIL

Characteristics:

Loamy soil is a balanced mixture of sand, silt, and clay, combining the best qualities of each. It has good drainage, moisture retention, and fertility, making it ideal for a wide variety of plants.

Impact on Survival Gardening:

• Advantages: Loamy soil supports healthy plant growth due to its excellent balance of drainage and moisture retention. It's also fertile and easy to work with.

• Challenges: Although loamy soil is ideal, it still requires regular maintenance to keep its optimal properties.

Improvement Strategies:

• Regularly add organic matter to maintain soil fertility and structure.

• Implement crop rotation to prevent nutrient depletion and maintain soil health.

SILTY SOIL

Characteristics:

Silty soil consists of fine particles that give it a smooth, soapy texture. It holds moisture well and is fertile but can become compacted and prone to erosion.

Impact on Survival Gardening:

• Advantages: Silty soil's high moisture and nutrient content make it conducive to plant growth.

• Challenges: It can compact easily, leading to poor aeration and potential erosion.

Improvement Strategies:

• Add organic matter to improve soil structure and prevent compaction.

• Use cover crops or mulch to protect the soil surface and reduce erosion.

PEATY SOIL

Characteristics:

Peaty soil is rich in organic matter and retains high moisture levels. It is typically found in wetlands and has a dark, spongy texture. Peaty soil tends to be acidic and may have low nutrient levels.

Impact on Survival Gardening:

• Advantages: High organic content improves fertility and moisture retention.

• Challenges: The acidic pH and potential nutrient deficiencies can limit plant growth.

Improvement Strategies:

- Adjust soil pH with lime if necessary to make it more suitable for a wider range of plants.

- Add balanced fertilizers to address nutrient deficiencies and support plant growth.

CHALKY SOIL

Characteristics:

Chalky soil has a high calcium carbonate content, making it alkaline. It is often stony and can be challenging to work with. This soil type can have high pH levels that affect nutrient availability.

Impact on Survival Gardening:

• Advantages: Good drainage and less prone to waterlogging.

• Challenges: Alkaline pH can limit nutrient availability and may make it difficult for some plants to thrive.

Improvement Strategies:

- Use soil acidifiers or organic matter to lower the pH and improve nutrient availability.

- Regularly add compost to enhance soil structure and fertility.

SALINE SOIL

Characteristics:

Saline soil contains high levels of soluble salts, which can be harmful to most plants. It is typically found in arid or semi-arid regions where evaporation exceeds precipitation, leading to salt accumulation. It can also be abundantly found along coastal areas where ocean sprays interact with the shore's soil chemistry and increase its saline content.

Impact on Survival Gardening:

- Advantages: May support salt-tolerant plants.
- Challenges: High salinity can lead to poor plant growth and soil degradation.

Improvement Strategies:

- Improve drainage and use leaching techniques to reduce salt concentration.
- Choose salt-tolerant crops or use soil amendments to mitigate the effects of salinity.

SOIL TESTING AND AMENDMENT

Testing and amending soil are crucial steps in ensuring that your garden provides the optimal conditions for plant growth. Proper testing helps identify nutrient deficiencies, pH imbalances, and other issues, while amending the soil improves its structure and fertility. Here we provide a detailed guide on how to test and amend soil effectively

TESTING SOIL

a. Collecting Soil Samples:

• Select Multiple Locations: To get an accurate representation of your garden soil, collect samples from several locations within your garden. Avoid areas that are atypical, such as where you've added large amounts of compost or where there might be contamination.

• Depth and Method: Using a garden trowel or soil probe, take samples from the top 6 to 8 inches of soil, which is where most plant roots will be. Place the soil in a clean bucket and mix it thoroughly.

b. Testing Soil pH:

• Home Testing Kits: Soil pH can be tested using a home testing kit, which typically includes a pH meter or test strips. Follow the kit's instructions for mixing soil with water and adding the testing solution.

• Professional Testing: For a more comprehensive analysis, send a sample to a local agricultural extension office or a soil testing laboratory. They provide detailed information on soil pH and can offer recommendations for amendments.

c. Testing Soil Nutrients:

• Soil Test Kits: These kits can also test for essential nutrients such as nitrogen, phosphorus, and potassium. They often include reagents and color charts to compare results.

- Professional Analysis: Laboratories offer more detailed nutrient analysis, including secondary and trace nutrients. This can help tailor your fertilization strategy more precisely.

d. Testing Soil Texture:

- Jar Test: To determine soil texture, fill a clear jar with soil and water, then shake it thoroughly. Let it settle for 24 hours. Sand will settle at the bottom, silt in the middle, and clay on top. Measure the proportions to determine your soil texture.

- Feel Test: You can also estimate soil texture by feel. Sandy soil feels gritty, clayey soil feels sticky, and loamy soil feels smooth and workable.

- Ribbon Test: Another method is the soil ribbon test. Take a ball of moist soil and press it between your thumb and pointer finger to form a ribbon. If no ribbon forms, the soil is sandy; if it forms a long ribbon, the soil is clayey; and if the ribbon is shorter and breaks easily, the soil contains more silt.

AMENDING SOIL

a. Improving Soil Structure:

- Organic Matter: Adding organic matter, such as compost, well-rotted manure, or leaf mold, improves soil structure, enhances drainage, and increases nutrient availability. Incorporate organic matter into the top 6 to 8 inches of soil.

- Mulch: Applying a layer of mulch (straw, wood chips, or leaf litter) on the soil surface helps retain moisture, regulate temperature, and reduce erosion. As it decomposes, it also adds organic matter to the soil.

b. Adjusting Soil pH:

• Raising pH (Decreasing Acidity): If your soil is too acidic (pH below 6.0), you can raise the pH by adding lime (calcium carbonate). For a more gradual approach, use dolomitic lime, which also provides magnesium. Follow the application rate suggested by your soil test results.

• Lowering pH (Increasing Acidity): If your soil is too alkaline (pH above 7.0), you can lower the pH by adding sulfur, peat moss, or pine needles. Elemental sulfur is commonly used for this purpose, but it should be applied carefully to avoid over-acidification.

c. Adding Nutrients:

• Fertilizers: Based on soil test results, apply fertilizers to address nutrient deficiencies. Use balanced fertilizers or those specifically formulated for the nutrients your soil lacks. Organic options include fish emulsion, bone meal, and blood meal.

• Green Manures and Cover Crops: Planting cover crops like clover or rye can add nutrients (such as nitrogen) to the soil and improve its structure. Green manures are grown during the off-season and then tilled into the soil.

d. Improving Drainage:

• Sand and Organic Matter: If your soil has poor drainage, especially if it's clayey, you can improve it by mixing in coarse sand and organic matter. This helps create larger soil particles that improve water movement.

• Raised Beds: For areas with persistent drainage problems, consider building raised beds. This elevates the planting area, enhances drainage, and allows for better control of soil conditions.

e. Enhancing Soil Fertility:

• Crop Rotation: Rotating crops each season can prevent nutrient depletion and reduce the risk of soil-borne diseases. Different crops have different nutrient needs, so rotating helps maintain a balanced soil nutrient profile.

• Composting: Maintain a compost pile or bin to continually add rich organic matter to your garden. Composting kitchen scraps, yard waste, and other organic materials provides a steady supply of nutrients and improves soil health.

f. Addressing Soil Compaction:

• Aeration: If your soil is compacted, use a garden fork or aerator to loosen it. This improves air and water movement and allows roots to penetrate more easily. Avoid working the soil when it's too wet to prevent further compaction.

• Cover Crops: Planting cover crops with deep root systems can help break up compacted soil and improve its structure over time.

ONGOING SOIL MANAGEMENT

a. Regular Testing: Periodically test your soil to monitor changes in pH and nutrient levels. This helps ensure that amendments and fertilization strategies remain effective and that soil health is maintained.

b. Continuous Improvement: Keep adding organic matter, practicing crop rotation, and adjusting pH and nutrients as needed to maintain optimal soil conditions. Healthy soil is a dynamic system that benefits from ongoing care and attention.

By regularly testing and amending your soil, you provide the best possible environment for your plants, leading to a more productive and resilient survival garden.

COMPOSTING FOR HEALTHY SOIL

Composting is an essential practice for cultivating healthy soil in a survival garden, offering numerous benefits that contribute to the garden's overall success and sustainability. Composting involves transforming organic waste—such as kitchen scraps and yard trimmings—into nutrient-rich compost, a dark, crumbly substance that enhances soil fertility and structure. This process is driven by microorganisms like bacteria and fungi, which break down complex organic materials into simpler forms that plants can readily absorb.

The benefits of composting are manifold: it improves soil texture by making it loamier, which in turn enhances its ability to retain moisture and nutrients. This is crucial for a survival garden, where the health of the soil directly impacts plant growth and productivity. Composting also promotes soil health by encouraging the presence of beneficial microbes and earthworms, which contribute to a vibrant soil ecosystem.

1 → To start composting, one must choose a method that suits their space and needs. Traditional compost piles, compost bins, vermicomposting, and Bokashi composting are all viable options, each with its unique advantages. For example, traditional piles are straightforward and cost-effective but require regular turning and management. Compost bins, on the other hand, help contain the composting process, keeping pests out and making maintenance easier. Vermicomposting, which uses worms to decompose organic matter, is ideal for small spaces and produces highly nutrient-dense vermicompost. Bokashi composting is another method that ferments organic waste using special microorganisms, allowing for the inclusion of materials like meat and dairy that are typically avoided in other composting methods.

2 → When setting up a compost system, selecting the right materials is crucial. Greens, such as vegetable scraps and coffee grounds, provide nitrogen and help heat up the compost, while browns, like dried leaves and cardboard, offer carbon and improve soil structure. Balancing these materials in the right ratio—typically about two parts browns to one part green—ensures efficient decomposition and reduces the risk of unpleasant odors. The compost pile should be kept moist, similar to a wrung-out sponge, and turned regularly to introduce air and maintain microbial activity. Proper aeration helps prevent the pile from becoming too compacted, which can slow down the decomposition process.

3 → Monitoring the compost pile involves checking its temperature, which should ideally reach between 130-160°F (54-71°C) to effectively kill pathogens and weed seeds. A well-maintained compost pile will have a pleasant, earthy smell; foul odors usually indicate an imbalance, such as excessive moisture or inadequate aeration. If the compost pile cools down, additional turning or materials may be needed to reignite microbial activity. Pests can be managed by avoiding problematic materials like meats and dairy, and using a bin or tumbler to keep pests at bay.

4 → Once the compost is ready, it should be dark, crumbly, and have an earthy aroma. This typically takes several months to a year, depending on the method and conditions. Harvesting compost involves removing the finished product from the bin or pile and incorporating it into garden beds or containers. Compost can also be used as mulch to conserve moisture and suppress weeds. Advanced techniques, such as making compost tea or using Bokashi composting, can further enhance soil fertility and productivity.

Overall, composting is a fundamental practice for building and maintaining healthy soil in a survival garden. It improves soil structure, provides essential nutrients, and supports a sustainable gardening approach by recycling organic waste. Understanding and applying composting principles effectively allow gardeners enhance soil health, boost plant growth, and contribute to a more environmentally friendly and self-sufficient gardening practice.

CHAPTER 5

WATER MANAGEMENT

Managing water properly in a survival garden is essential to maintaining the health and productivity of your plants, especially when water resources are limited or unreliable. The first step in effective water management is understanding your garden's specific needs. Different plants require varying amounts of water, and soil types can influence how quickly water is absorbed or retained. For example, sandy soils drain water rapidly, necessitating more frequent watering, while clay soils retain water longer but can become waterlogged, harming plant roots.

Efficient watering techniques are needed in a survival garden. Traditional methods like overhead sprinklers often result in significant water loss due to evaporation and can promote the spread of diseases by wetting the foliage. Instead, consider using drip irrigation or soaker hoses, which deliver water directly to the base of the plants, minimizing evaporation and ensuring that water reaches the roots where it's needed most. Watering in the early morning when temperatures are cooler can further reduce evaporation, making your water use more efficient. While watering late in the evening is possible, it can increase the risk of fungal problems due to prolonged moisture on the plant and soil overnight. Watering in the early morning is preferable, as it allows the soil and plants to dry out with the sun, reducing the likelihood of disease.

Mulching is another key strategy for conserving water in a survival garden. It involves spreading a layer of organic material like straw, wood chips, or leaf litter over the soil surface, this can significantly reduce moisture loss through evaporation, keep the soil cooler, and suppress weeds that would otherwise compete with your plants for water. Organic mulches have the added benefit of decomposing over time, enriching the soil with nutrients and improving its ability to retain moisture.

Harvesting rainwater is an excellent way to reduce your reliance on municipal water supplies and ensure you have a steady water source for your garden. Installing rain barrels or larger cisterns to collect runoff from your roof provides a free, sustainable source of water that can be used during dry periods. Choose roofing materials that won't leach harmful substances into the water. Ideal options include metal roofs (such as galvanized steel or aluminum with food-grade coatings), clay or slate tiles, and untreated wood. These materials are non-toxic and suitable for collecting clean water.

On the other hand, materials like asphalt shingles, treated or painted wood, copper, and PVC with harmful additives should be avoided. These can leach chemicals that contaminate the water, posing risks to both plants and human health.

Rainwater is naturally soft and free of chemicals like chlorine, making it ideal for watering plants. To maximize the benefits of rainwater harvesting, ensure your barrels are covered to prevent debris from entering and to reduce evaporation.

Choosing water-wise gardening practices is also vital for managing water efficiently. This involves selecting plants that are well-suited to your local climate and require less water. Native plants or those adapted to your region are typically more drought-tolerant and can thrive with minimal watering once established. Additionally, grouping plants with similar water needs together, known as hydrozoning, can help you water more efficiently and avoid overwatering certain areas of your garden.

Improving soil quality is another aspect of water management. Soil rich in organic matter holds moisture more effectively, reducing the need for frequent watering. Adding compost or well-rotted manure to your soil enhances its structure, increases its water-holding capacity, and improves nutrient availability for plants. For sandy soils, adding organic matter helps retain water, while for clay soils, it improves drainage and prevents waterlogging. The goal is to create a balanced soil environment that provides plants with a steady supply of moisture.

To further minimize water waste, use watering techniques that deliver water directly to the plant roots. Creating small basins or berms around the base of plants can help capture water and prevent runoff. Deep watering encourages roots to grow deeper into the soil, making plants more drought-resistant. Shallow watering often leads to shallow root systems that are more vulnerable to drought conditions.

EFFICIENT IRRIGATION TECHNIQUES

Efficient irrigation techniques are essential for maintaining a healthy and productive survival garden while minimizing water waste. These methods ensure that water is delivered directly to the roots of your plants, where it is needed most, reducing evaporation and runoff. Here's a look at some of the most effective irrigation techniques you can implement in your survival garden:

1. Drip Irrigation

Drip irrigation is one of the most efficient watering methods available, particularly for a survival garden. This system delivers water directly to the base of each plant through a network of tubes, pipes, and emitters. The slow and steady release of water ensures that it penetrates deep into the soil, reaching the root zone without any excess runoff or evaporation. Drip irrigation can be customized to suit different garden layouts and plant types, making it ideal for both small and large gardens. Moreover, it allows for precise control over the amount of water each plant receives, which is especially important for plants with varying water needs.

To set up a drip irrigation system, you'll need a main water supply line, distribution tubing, emitters, and connectors. The system can be automated with a timer to water at optimal times, such as early morning or late evening when temperatures are cooler, reducing evaporation. Drip irrigation not only conserves water but also keeps foliage dry, which helps prevent fungal diseases that thrive in wet conditions.

2. Soaker Hoses

Soaker hoses are another efficient irrigation option, especially for garden beds, rows of plants, or areas with dense plantings. These hoses are made of porous material that allows water to seep out slowly along the entire length of the hose. Like drip irrigation, soaker hoses deliver water directly to the soil surface, where it can be absorbed by the roots without wasting water through evaporation or runoff.

Soaker hoses are easy to install and can be laid out in straight lines, curves, or around the base of plants. They work well in conjunction with mulch, which helps retain soil moisture and further reduces evaporation. To use soaker hoses effectively, run them for a set period, typically 30 minutes to an hour, depending on the soil type and plant needs. Using a timer can help ensure consistent watering.

3. Mulched Basin Irrigation

Mulched basin irrigation involves creating small basins or depressions around the base of each plant and filling these basins with water. The basins are then covered with mulch to slow evaporation and keep the soil cool. This method is particularly effective for trees, shrubs, and larger plants that require deep watering. The water collected in the basins slowly seeps into the soil, providing moisture directly to the root zone.

This technique is simple to implement and requires minimal equipment. Mulching the basin conserves water and also improves soil structure and nutrient content as the mulch breaks down. Mulched basin irrigation is especially useful in areas with limited water availability, as it ensures that every drop of water is used efficiently.

4. Furrow Irrigation

Furrow irrigation is a traditional method often used in larger vegetable gardens or fields. It involves creating shallow trenches, or furrows, between rows of plants and flooding these furrows with water. The water then seeps into the soil and spreads out to irrigate the roots of the plants on either side. Furrow irrigation can be an efficient technique when used correctly, particularly in soils with good water-holding capacity.

To maximize efficiency with furrow irrigation, it's important to level the furrows to prevent uneven water distribution and reduce runoff. The use of mulch in the furrows can also help retain moisture and minimize evaporation. While furrow irrigation is less precise than drip irrigation, it can still be an effective way to water large areas of a survival garden when water is delivered at a controlled rate.

5. Wicking Beds

Wicking beds are an innovative irrigation method that uses a self-watering system to keep plants hydrated. These beds are designed with a reservoir at the bottom, which is filled with water. The soil above the reservoir draws up water through capillary action, effectively "wicking" moisture up to the plant roots as needed. This method is highly efficient because it delivers water directly to the root zone and reduces surface evaporation.

Wicking beds are particularly beneficial in arid regions or areas with limited water availability. They require less frequent watering and can even be left unattended for longer periods, making them ideal for survival gardening. To set up a wicking bed, you'll need a waterproof container or liner, a reservoir layer (such as gravel or sand), and a soil layer. The key is to maintain the reservoir with enough water to keep the wicking process active.

6. Ollas (Clay Pot Irrigation)

Ollas are ancient clay pots that provide a simple yet effective irrigation method. These unglazed pots are buried in the soil with just the neck exposed. The olla is filled with water, which slowly seeps out through the porous clay, hydrating the surrounding soil. Plants draw water from the soil as needed, creating a highly efficient, self-regulating watering system.

Ollas are particularly useful for small gardens or individual plants, such as vegetables or herbs. They help conserve water by delivering it directly to the root zone and reduce the frequency of watering. The use of ollas also minimizes weed growth, as the surrounding soil remains relatively dry. Ollas are easy to use and can be refilled as needed, making them a great option for sustainable, low-maintenance irrigation.

7. Rainwater Harvesting and Gravity-Fed Irrigation

Rainwater harvesting involves collecting and storing rainwater for later use in your garden. This water can be distributed through a gravity-fed irrigation system, which relies on gravity to move water from a higher point (such as a rain barrel or cistern) to the garden. This method eliminates the need for pumps and electricity, making it an eco-friendly and efficient way to irrigate a survival garden.

To set up a gravity-fed irrigation system, you'll need to place your water storage container at an elevated position, connect it to a hose or drip line, and let gravity do the work. This method is particularly effective in areas with irregular rainfall, allowing you to make the most of natural water sources. Combining rainwater harvesting with drip irrigation or soaker hoses can further increase efficiency and sustainability.

8. Subsurface Irrigation

Subsurface irrigation involves placing irrigation lines below the soil surface, directly delivering water to the root zone. This method minimizes evaporation and runoff, making it one of the most water-efficient irrigation techniques available. Subsurface irrigation is ideal for perennial crops, lawns, and areas with sandy soils that drain quickly.

The installation of subsurface irrigation systems can be more complex and costly compared to other methods, but the long-term water savings and improved plant health often justify the investment.

9. Hand Watering with Care

While not as automated as other methods, hand watering can be an efficient way to irrigate a small survival garden, especially when done with attention to detail. Using a watering can or a hose fitted with a nozzle that delivers a gentle spray allows you to target the base of each plant, minimizing water waste. Hand watering also gives you the opportunity to inspect your plants for signs of stress, pests, or disease.

To make hand watering more efficient, water in the early morning when temperatures are cooler, reducing evaporation. Once again, avoid watering in the evening as it can lead to fungal growth. Water deeply but infrequently to encourage deep root growth, which makes plants more resilient to drought.

10. Incorporating Smart Irrigation Technology

For those who want to take irrigation efficiency to the next level, smart irrigation technology offers advanced solutions. These systems use sensors to monitor soil moisture, weather conditions, and plant water needs, adjusting the watering schedule accordingly. Smart irrigation controllers can be programmed to water specific zones at optimal times, ensuring that each area of your garden receives the right amount of water without any waste.

While smart irrigation systems represent a higher upfront cost, they can significantly reduce water usage and ensure that your survival garden remains healthy and productive with minimal manual intervention.

RAINWATER HARVESTING

Rainwater harvesting is the process of collecting and storing rainwater for later use, rather than allowing it to run off and be lost. This method is especially valuable in regions where water is scarce, unreliable, or expensive. The collected rainwater can be used for a variety of purposes, including irrigation, drinking, washing, and even replenishing groundwater supplies.

In its simplest form, rainwater harvesting involves capturing runoff from rooftops made from non-toxic, viable materials like metal roofs (such as galvanized steel or aluminum with food-grade coatings), clay or slate tiles, and untreated wood, which is then transported via gutters and directed into storage containers like barrels, cisterns, or tanks. In all cases, rooftops made from asphalt shingles will create long-term toxicity in the edibles' growth, and so this material must be avoided. More complex systems might include filtration and purification processes, making the water suitable for drinking and other household uses. The concept isn't new; it's been practiced for thousands of years in different cultures around the world, particularly in arid and semi-arid regions where water is precious.

WHY RAINWATER HARVESTING IS IMPORTANT

Rainwater harvesting is a sustainable and practical solution for managing water resources. It helps reduce reliance on municipal water supplies, lowers utility bills, and provides a backup water source during droughts or periods of low rainfall. In areas where water infrastructure is lacking or aging, harvesting rainwater can serve as a critical resource, ensuring that communities and individuals have access to water even when traditional sources are unavailable or unreliable.

Moreover, rainwater is naturally soft and free from many of the chemicals and salts found in groundwater or tap water, making it better for plants, especially in gardens. It can be particularly beneficial in survival gardening, where efficient water use is key to maintaining a productive garden under challenging conditions.

WHEN RAINWATER HARVESTING BECOMES NECESSARY

Rainwater harvesting becomes necessary in several scenarios:

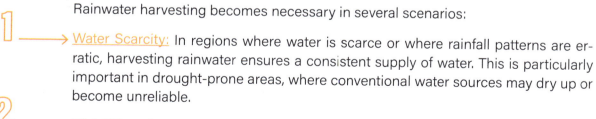

1. → Water Scarcity: In regions where water is scarce or where rainfall patterns are erratic, harvesting rainwater ensures a consistent supply of water. This is particularly important in drought-prone areas, where conventional water sources may dry up or become unreliable.

2. → High Water Costs: In areas where the cost of water is high, collecting rainwater can significantly reduce water bills. This is especially beneficial for those who rely heavily on water for gardening, farming, or other outdoor activities.

3. → Inadequate Water Infrastructure: In rural or undeveloped areas where water infra-

structure is either non-existent or poorly maintained, rainwater harvesting provides an independent water supply. This can be crucial for households that do not have access to a reliable municipal water system.

5 ⟶ Environmental Considerations: Rainwater harvesting is also an eco-friendly practice that reduces the demand on overburdened water resources. It helps reduce runoff, which can lead to soil erosion, flooding, and the contamination of local waterways with pollutants.

6 ⟶ Emergency Preparedness: Having a rainwater harvesting system in place can be a vital part of emergency preparedness. In the event of a natural disaster or other emergencies that disrupt water supplies, stored rainwater can provide a critical backup for drinking, cooking, and sanitation needs.

7 ⟶ Survival Gardening: For survival gardening, rainwater harvesting is essential backup. It ensures that the garden remains irrigated without depleting other water sources, which might be needed for drinking or other essential uses. During prolonged dry periods, having a reserve of harvested rainwater can make the difference between a thriving garden and withering plot.

HOW TO IMPLEMENT RAINWATER HARVESTING

To set up a basic rainwater harvesting system, you'll need a few key components:

- Catchment Area: Typically, this is your roof, which will collect rainwater and channel it into the system. The size and material of the roof will affect how much water you can collect.

- Gutters and Downspouts: These direct water from the roof into your storage container. It's important to keep these clean and free of debris to ensure the smooth flow of water.

- First Flush Diverter: This is a device that diverts the initial flow of water, which may contain contaminants like dust and bird droppings, away from your storage container. This helps keep your stored water cleaner.

- **Storage Containers:** These can range from simple rain barrels to large cisterns, depending on your water needs and available space. The containers should be covered to prevent contamination and evaporation. As a bonus, you can house goldfish in uncovered water storage to control mosquito growth since they feed on their larvae, keeping the water safer and mosquito-free. The goldfish need to be transferred once the monsoons pass.

- **Filtration and Purification Systems:** If you plan to use the rainwater for drinking or other household uses, you'll need to filter and purify it. This can be done using a combination of mesh screens, charcoal filters, UV sterilizers, and other purification methods.

- **Distribution System:** Once collected, the rainwater needs to be distributed to where it's needed, such as your garden. This can be done using gravity-fed systems, pumps, or simple watering cans.

MANAGING WATER RESOURCES IN DROUGHT

Managing water resources when water is scarce is a crucial skill, especially in areas prone to drought or where water supplies are unreliable. It involves not just careful planning and conservation, but also adopting practices that maximize the efficiency of every drop. If you're managing a household without 24/7 water, a farmstead, or a survival garden, water resources management is indispensable

UNDERSTANDING WATER NEEDS AND PRIORITIZATION

The first step in managing scarce water resources is understanding the specific needs of your household, garden, or farm. During times of scarcity, prioritizing essential uses becomes necessary. For instance, drinking water and sanitation should always come first, followed by water for food production, and then non-essential uses like landscaping or recreational activities.

In a garden or farm setting, this means prioritizing water for crops that provide the most nutrition or have the highest value. Drought-tolerant plants, which require less water to thrive, should be given priority over those that are water-intensive.

WATER CONSERVATION TECHNIQUES

Conservation is at the heart of managing water scarcity. Simple changes in behavior and the adoption of water-saving practices can significantly reduce water usage:

1.   **Fix Leaks:** One of the simplest yet most effective conservation methods is fixing leaks in pipes, faucets, and irrigation systems. A small drip can waste a surprising amount of water over time, so regular maintenance is key.

2.   **Use Water-Saving Fixtures:** Installing low-flow faucets, showerheads, and toilets can reduce water consumption in the household by significant amounts. These fixtures are designed to use less water without sacrificing performance.

3.   **Shorten Showers and Reduce Bathing Frequency:** In times of extreme scarcity, consider reducing the frequency of bathing or opting for shorter showers. This can save gallons of water daily.

4.   **Reuse Greywater:** Greywater is lightly used water from sinks, showers, and washing machines. With proper filtration and treatment, it can be reused for irrigation or toilet flushing, reducing the demand for fresh water.

5.   **Install Water Meters:** Keeping track of water usage with a meter can help identify where conservation efforts should be focused. Being aware of how much water is being used can encourage more mindful usage.

EFFICIENT IRRIGATION PRACTICES

In a garden or agricultural context, efficient irrigation is crucial when water is scarce. This involves adopting methods that deliver water directly to the plants' roots, where it is needed most, and minimizing waste

1.   **Drip Irrigation:** As mentioned earlier, drip irrigation systems deliver water slowly and directly to the plant roots, significantly reducing evaporation and runoff. This method is particularly effective in arid regions or during drought conditions.

2.   **Soaker Hoses:** Soaker hoses work similarly to drip irrigation, allowing water to seep out slowly along their length. They are ideal for watering rows of plants or garden beds without wasting water on unneeded areas.

3.   **Mulching:** Applying mulch around plants helps to retain soil moisture by reducing evaporation. Organic mulches, such as straw, wood chips, or leaves, can also improve soil health as they decompose.

4.   **Watering at the Right Time:** Watering during the early morning or late evening when temperatures are cooler can reduce water loss due to evaporation. This practice ensures that more water is available for plant absorption.

5.   **Hydrozoning:** Grouping plants with similar water needs together, known as hydrozoning, allows you to water more efficiently. This prevents overwatering or underwatering specific areas of your garden.

ALTERNATIVE WATER SOURCES

In some cases, alternative water sources may be necessary to supplement your supply:

1. Greywater Systems: As previously mentioned, greywater from household activities can be treated and reused. Setting up a greywater system requires careful planning to ensure that the water is safe for its intended use, particularly for irrigation.

2. Desalination: In coastal areas, desalination plants can convert seawater into freshwater. While energy-intensive and costly, desalination is a viable option where freshwater sources are extremely limited.

3. Water Recycling: Water recycling involves treating wastewater to make it reusable. This can range from simple filtration for irrigation to more advanced purification for drinking water.

DROUGHT-RESISTANT PLANTS AND LANDSCAPING

In regions prone to water scarcity, planting drought-resistant plants is an effective way to reduce water usage. Native plants, which are adapted to local conditions, often require less water and maintenance. Additionally, xeriscaping—landscaping designed to reduce the need for irrigation—can create attractive, low-water gardens that are both functional and sustainable.

Xeriscaping involves using drought-tolerant plants, such as succulents, cacti, and other water-efficient species, along with techniques like mulching and soil improvement to minimize water use. This type of landscaping not only conserves water but also reduces the time and resources needed to maintain the garden.

WATER RATIONING AND EMERGENCY PLANNING

In severe drought conditions, rationing water may become necessary. This involves allocating water based on priority needs and carefully monitoring usage to ensure that essential tasks are met without exceeding available supplies. Emergency water storage, such as large cisterns or tanks, should be part of your preparedness plan, ensuring that you have a backup supply for critical needs.

When planning for water scarcity, it's important to have a clear understanding of your daily water usage and how much is available. This will allow you to make informed decisions about where to cut back and how to best allocate resources. In extreme cases, you may need to implement strict water-saving measures, such as limiting showers, reducing laundry frequency, or even using disposable dishes to minimize washing.

COMMUNITY AND POLICY INVOLVEMENT

Managing water scarcity is also a community issue. Participating in local water conservation programs, advocating for sustainable water management policies, and working with neighbors to implement community-wide conservation measures can help ensure that everyone has access to water during times of scarcity.

On a larger scale, supporting policies that promote water conservation, such as restrictions on water usage during droughts, incentives for installing water-efficient appliances, or investments in infrastructure improvements, can help address water scarcity more effectively.

CHAPTER 6

BUILDING GARDEN STRUCTURES

Building garden structures is a gratifying endeavor that enhances both the functionality and visual appeal of your garden. Each garden structure serves a unique purpose and requires an approach unique to you, from designing and constructing to maintaining.

RAISED BEDS AND CONTAINER GARDENING

RAISED BEDS: AN OVERVIEW

Benefits

Raised beds are essentially garden beds that are elevated above the surrounding soil level. They can be built from a variety of materials, including wood, metal, or stone, and they offer several key advantages. One of the primary benefits is improved soil drainage. Because raised beds are elevated, excess water can drain away more easily, which helps prevent waterlogged soil and root rot. Additionally, raised beds allow for better soil control, as you can fill them with a custom soil mix tailored to the needs of your plants. This makes it easier to grow plants in areas with poor native soil.

Raised beds also reduce the need for bending over, making gardening more accessible for individuals with mobility issues. They can be built to a comfortable height, which reduces strain on the back and knees. Furthermore, raised beds can help with weed control and pest management. By creating a defined growing area, weeds are easier to manage, and the elevated design can deter some pests.

Setup:

1. To build a raised bed, start by selecting a location that receives adequate sunlight and has good access to water.

2. Measure and cut your materials to the desired size. Common dimensions for raised beds are 4x8 feet or 4x4 feet, but you can customize these based on your space.

3. Assemble the frame by securing the corners with screws or nails.

4. _____ Place the frame on level ground, and fill it with a mixture of topsoil and compost. The height of the bed can vary, but a depth of 12 to 18 inches is typically sufficient for most plants.

5. _____ Once filled, your raised bed is ready for planting.

Maintenance:

Raised beds require regular maintenance to keep them in optimal condition. This includes monitoring soil moisture levels, adding compost or organic matter to replenish nutrients, and checking for signs of pests or diseases. Mulching can help retain soil moisture and suppress weeds. During the growing season, ensure that your plants are receiving adequate water and nutrients, and consider rotating crops to prevent soil depletion and reduce pest problems.

CONTAINER GARDENING: AN OVERVIEW

Container gardening involves growing plants in pots or other containers rather than directly in the ground. This method is particularly advantageous for those with limited space, such as apartment dwellers or those with small yards. Containers can be placed on balconies, patios, or windowsills, making it possible to grow a wide variety of plants in confined spaces. Additionally, container gardening offers excellent control over soil quality and drainage, as you can use specific potting mixes tailored to the needs of your plants.

Containers also make it easy to move plants around, which is useful for adjusting their exposure to sunlight or protecting them from harsh weather conditions. This mobility is especially beneficial for seasonal plants or those that require specific growing conditions. Container gardening can also reduce the risk of soil-borne diseases and pests, as the soil is contained and less likely to be contaminated by external sources.

1. When starting with container gardening, choose containers that are appropriate for the size and type of plants you want to grow.

2. Ensure that containers have drainage holes to prevent water from accumulating at the bottom, which can lead to root rot.

3. Use a high-quality potting mix designed for container gardening, as it provides the necessary aeration and drainage that plants need.

4. Fill the container with the potting mix, leaving some space at the top for watering.

5. Before using any container, clean and sterilize it to reduce pests and plant diseases. Soak the pots in water with a capful of bleach for 5 to 10 minutes, scrub to remove dirt, and rinse thoroughly with clean water. Set the pots out in the sun to dry, allowing the sunlight to sterilize anything missed. This step is essential for both old and new pots.

6. Plant your seeds or seedlings according to the recommended depth and spacing.

Maintenance:

Container gardens require regular maintenance to ensure healthy plant growth. This includes monitoring soil moisture levels, as containers can dry out more quickly than garden beds. Water plants consistently, but avoid overwatering, which can lead to root rot. Fertilize regularly, as container soil can become depleted of nutrients more rapidly than garden soil. Also, check for signs of pests or diseases and take appropriate action if needed. Containers may need to be moved or rotated to ensure that plants receive adequate sunlight and protection from the elements.

COMPARING RAISED BEDS AND CONTAINER GARDENING

Comparing Raised Beds and Container Gardening

Both raised beds and container gardening offer flexibility and control over your growing environment, but they cater to different needs and preferences:

- Space: Raised beds are ideal for those with a bit of garden space, providing a larger growing area and the ability to grow a variety of plants. Containers, on the other hand, are perfect for smaller spaces and can be used to grow plants in a more compact area.

- Soil and Drainage: Raised beds allow for better soil control and drainage, making them suitable for areas with poor native soil. Containers also offer excellent control over soil quality and drainage but require careful attention to prevent waterlogging.

- Accessibility: Raised beds can be built to a comfortable height, reducing strain on the body. Containers are portable and can be placed at a convenient height or moved as needed, but they may require more frequent maintenance to manage soil moisture and nutrient levels.

- Plant Variety: Raised beds are versatile and can accommodate a wide range of plants, including root vegetables, leafy greens, and flowering plants. Containers are well-suited for smaller plants, herbs, and compact varieties of vegetables and flowers.

TRELLISES AND SUPPORTS

Trellises are structures designed to support climbing plants by providing a framework for them to grow upward. They come in various shapes and sizes, from simple flat panels to elaborate arches and obelisks. Common materials for trellises include wood, metal, plastic, and bamboo. The design of a trellis ranges from minimalist to decorative, depending on your garden's aesthetic and functional needs. Trellises are often used for plants like peas, beans, cucumbers, and certain flowering vines, helping to keep these plants off the ground and making them easier to manage and harvest.

Supports, on the other hand, are typically simpler structures that help individual plants grow upright. They can include stakes, cages, or rings. Supports are particularly useful for plants with heavy fruits or flowers, like tomatoes and peppers, which can benefit from additional stability. Supports are generally used in combination with trellises or alone, depending on the type of plant and its growth habit.

BENEFITS OF USING TRELLISES AND SUPPORTS

1. **Maximize Space:** Trellises and supports allow plants to grow vertically, freeing up valuable ground space for other plants. This is especially beneficial in small gardens or container gardens where space is limited.

2. **Improve Air Circulation:** Trellises and supports improve air circulation around the foliage because the plants are elevated off the ground. This helps reduce the risk of fungal diseases and encourages healthier plant growth.

3. **Enhance Sun Exposure:** Vertical growth ensures that plants receive more uniform sunlight. Climbing plants on a trellis can get better light exposure compared to those growing on the ground, which may be shaded by other plants or structures.

4. **Ease of Harvesting:** Plants grown on trellises or supports are easier to access and harvest. This can be particularly helpful for vining crops that can become tangled or difficult to reach when grown on the ground.

5. **Reduce Pest and Disease Issues:** Elevated plants are less likely to come into contact with soil-borne pests and diseases. This can lead to healthier plants and potentially higher yields.

BUILDING AND INSTALLING TRELLISES

1. The first step in building a trellis is to design it based on the types of plants you plan to grow and the space available. Consider the height and width of the trellis to accommodate the plant's growth. Simple trellis designs include flat panels, A-frames, and leaning trellises. More elaborate designs might include arched structures or decorative latticework.

2. Choose materials that are durable and suited to your garden environment. Wood is a popular choice for its versatility and natural look, while metal and plastic offer durability and low maintenance. Ensure that the materials are weather-resistant, especially if the trellis will be exposed to rain and sun.

3. Begin by measuring and cutting the materials to the desired dimensions. Assemble the frame using screws, nails, or bolts. For a simple flat trellis, attach horizontal slats or wire to the vertical supports. For an A-frame, connect the two sides at the top and secure them with braces. Ensure that the structure is stable and well-anchored.

4. Place the trellis in a location that provides adequate sunlight for the plants you intend to grow. Secure the base of the trellis in the ground or attach it to a wall or fence for added stability. Make sure the trellis is upright and level before planting.

5. As your plants grow, gently guide them onto the trellis using soft ties or twine. Regularly check the plants and adjust the ties as needed to ensure they are growing properly and not becoming tangled.

TYPES OF SUPPORTS AND THEIR USE

1.   **Stakes:** Stakes are simple, vertical supports that are driven into the ground next to the plant. They are commonly used for plants like tomatoes and peppers. Stakes can be made from wood, metal, or bamboo. Secure the plant to the stake with ties or clips, ensuring that the plant remains upright and supported as it grows.

2.   **Cages:** Plant cages are circular or square structures that encircle the plant, providing support for its growth. They are especially useful for tomatoes and other plants with heavy fruits. Cages can be made from wire or metal and should be placed around the plant early in the growing season to prevent damage to the roots.

3.   **Rings and Hoops:** Rings or hoops can be used to provide support for plants that need additional stability. These structures are often made from metal or plastic and are placed around the base of the plant. They are useful for supporting plants with tall, heavy growth.

4.   **Netting:** Netting can be stretched between stakes or attached to a trellis to provide support for climbing plants. It is particularly useful for beans and cucumbers, allowing them to climb and spread out without becoming tangled.

MAINTENANCE AND CARE

Regularly check the trellises and supports for signs of wear or damage. Ensure that the structure remains stable and secure, and make any necessary repairs or adjustments.

As plants grow, adjust ties and supports to accommodate their increasing size. Avoid tying plants too tightly, as this can damage the stems or restrict growth.

Keep trellises and supports clean and free of debris. Remove any dead plant material and check for signs of pests or diseases. Regular maintenance will help prolong the life of your garden structures and ensure they continue to function effectively.

In colder climates, consider removing or storing trellises and supports during the winter months to prevent damage from frost and snow. In warmer climates, ensure that structures are adequately anchored and resistant to sun damage.

GREENHOUSES AND COLD FRAMES

Greenhouses and cold frames are vital tools for gardeners who want to take control of their growing environment and extend their gardening season. A greenhouse is a larger, enclosed structure made of materials like glass, plastic, or polycarbonate, designed to trap heat and create a stable environment for plants. It allows gardeners to grow a variety of plants year-round, regardless of the external weather conditions.

Greenhouses make it possible to cultivate plants that wouldn't normally survive in your region's climate. Inside a greenhouse, you can control temperature, humidity, and light levels, which means you can grow tropical plants in a temperate zone or start your vegetable garden earlier in the season.

The benefits of a greenhouse are immense: extended growing seasons, the ability to grow more delicate or exotic plants, and a controlled environment that can lead to higher yields and healthier plants. However, setting up a greenhouse requires careful planning, from selecting the right location with maximum sunlight exposure to choosing materials that can withstand the local weather conditions. It's an investment of both time and resources, but for those who are serious about gardening, a greenhouse can be a game-changer.

On the other hand, a cold frame is a simpler and more cost-effective solution for extending the growing season. Essentially, a cold frame is a low, rectangular structure with a transparent lid, often made from repurposed materials like old windows. It's designed to protect plants from cold weather by trapping solar heat, creating a microclimate that is a few degrees warmer than the outside air.

This makes cold frames perfect for hardening off seedlings, starting plants earlier in the spring, or extending the harvest of cool-season crops like lettuce and spinach into the fall. Cold frames are easy to build and require minimal maintenance, making them accessible to gardeners with limited space or those who don't want to commit to the expense of a full greenhouse.

While they don't offer the same level of control as a greenhouse, cold frames are incredibly effective at what they do, providing just enough protection to keep plants growing through the colder seasons. They're also portable, so you can move them around your garden as needed to optimize sunlight exposure.

Whichever one you choose, a greenhouse or a cold frame, it depends largely on your gardening goals, available space, and budget. Greenhouses are ideal for those looking to garden year-round and experiment with a wider variety of plants, offering more control and versatility. Cold frames, while more limited, are perfect for gardeners who want a straightforward way to protect plants from early or late-season frosts without the commitment of a larger structure.

Both options offer significant advantages in extending your gardening season and protecting your plants, helping you make the most of your garden, no matter the weather.

PART 2
GROWING YOUR CROPS

CHAPTER

CHOOSING THE RIGHT PLANTS

ESSENTIAL SURVIVAL CROPS

Essential survival crops are those that provide maximum nutrition, are relatively easy to grow and store, and can sustain you through tough times when food might be scarce. These crops are often chosen for their high caloric value, long shelf life, and the ability to thrive in various conditions. They are the backbone of a survival garden because they can provide a reliable food source in case of emergencies, whether due to natural disasters, economic hardship, or other crises. Understanding what makes these crops essential is key to planning a garden that can sustain you and your family over the long term.

Root Vegetables: Root vegetables like potatoes, sweet potatoes, carrots, and beets are top contenders in any survival garden. Potatoes, in particular, are a powerhouse of nutrition, providing carbohydrates, vitamins, and minerals that are essential for maintaining energy levels. They are easy to grow, even in challenging soil conditions, and can be stored for months in a cool, dark place without spoiling. Sweet potatoes add variety and are packed with vitamins A and C, along with fiber. Carrots and beets are not only nutritious but also versatile in the kitchen. They can be eaten raw, cooked, or preserved, making them invaluable for long-term food security.

Legumes: Beans, peas, and lentils are crucial for their high protein content, which is often lacking in other survival crops. Legumes are also rich in fiber, iron, and B vitamins, making them an excellent choice for maintaining overall health. They can be grown in a variety of climates, and once dried, they have an incredibly long shelf life. Legumes are also beneficial to your garden because they fix nitrogen in the soil, improving fertility for other crops. This dual benefit makes them a cornerstone of any survival garden.

Grains: Corn, wheat, and oats are among the most essential grains you can grow in a survival garden. Corn is a versatile crop that can be used fresh, dried, or ground into flour. It's a high-yield crop, meaning it produces a lot of food per plant, and it's relatively easy to grow in most climates. Wheat is another staple, providing flour for bread, pasta, and other essential foods. While it requires more space and time to grow, the payoff in terms of food security is significant. Oats are a great addition for their nutritional value, particularly for breakfast foods, and they can be grown in less fertile soils where other crops might struggle.

Leafy Greens: Leafy greens like kale, spinach, and Swiss chard are vital for their high vitamin content, especially vitamins A, C, and K, as well as minerals like calcium and iron. These crops grow quickly, often within a few weeks, and can be harvested multiple times throughout the season, providing a continuous supply of fresh greens. They are also relatively easy to grow, even in small spaces or containers, making them accessible to gardeners of all levels. While they don't store as well as root vegetables or grains, they can be dehydrated or fermented to extend their shelf life.

Alliums: Onions, garlic, and leeks are part of the allium family, and they are indispensable in a survival garden. These crops add flavor to meals and are rich in antioxidants, which can help boost the immune system. Garlic, in particular, is known for its medicinal properties, including antibacterial and antiviral effects, making it a valuable addition to your diet during times of illness. Onions and garlic are relatively easy to grow and can be stored for several months if cured properly. They also help deter pests in the garden, making them beneficial companions to other crops.

Squash and Pumpkins: Winter squash and pumpkins are essential survival crops because of their long storage life and nutritional content. They are rich in vitamins

A and C, potassium, and fiber, and they can be stored for months in a cool, dry place. These crops are relatively easy to grow and produce large fruits that can feed a family for several meals. They can be used in a variety of dishes, from soups and stews to baked goods, providing versatility in your diet.

7 → **Perennial Vegetables:** Perennial vegetables like asparagus, rhubarb, and Jerusalem artichokes are valuable because they come back year after year without needing to be replanted. Asparagus, for example, is a springtime favorite that is packed with vitamins and minerals. While it takes a couple of years to establish, once it does, it will provide a reliable crop each season. Jerusalem artichokes, also known as sunchokes, are a tuber that is high in inulin, a type of carbohydrate that can help regulate blood sugar levels. These perennials add diversity to your survival garden and reduce the need for replanting, saving time and effort.

8 → **Herbs and Medicinal Plants:** Herbs like basil, thyme, rosemary, and medicinal plants like echinacea and calendula are important for flavoring food and for their health benefits. Many herbs have antibacterial, antiviral, and anti-inflammatory properties, which can be crucial during times when medical supplies might be limited. Herbs are also relatively easy to grow, often thriving in pots or small garden beds, and they can be dried and stored for long periods. Including a variety of herbs in your survival garden not only enhances the flavor of your meals but also provides natural remedies for common ailments.

9 → **Fruit Trees and Bushes:** While not as quick to establish, fruit trees like apple, pear, and cherry, along with bushes like blueberries and raspberries, are excellent long-term investments for a survival garden. Once mature, these plants can produce fruit for many years with minimal care. They provide essential vitamins and fiber, and the fruits can be eaten fresh, dried, or preserved as jams and jellies. Fruit trees and bushes also contribute to the biodiversity of your garden, attracting pollinators and other beneficial wildlife.

10 → **Hardy Vegetables:** Cabbage, broccoli, and Brussels sprouts are hardy vegetables that can withstand cooler temperatures, making them ideal for extending the growing season into the colder months. These crops are packed with nutrients, including vitamins C and K, fiber, and antioxidants. They can be grown in early spring or late fall when other crops might not thrive, ensuring a continuous food supply. Cabbage, in particular, can be stored for several weeks and is the primary ingredient in sauerkraut, a fermented food that is excellent for gut health.

COMPANION PLANTING

CARROTS — ✓ Beans, Garden peas, Lettuce, Onions, Tomatoes — ⊘ Drill, Parsnip, Parsley

CORN — ✓ Beans, Cucumbers, Garden peas, Melons, Potatoes, Squash — ⊘ Tomatoes

GARLIC — ✓ Beets, Carrots, Corn, Eggplant, Radishes, spinach — ✓ Tomatoes, Cucumbers, Pepper — ⊘ Beans, Gareden peas

ONIONS — ✓ Beets, Carrots, Cole crops, Lettuce — ⊘ Beans, Peas

PEPPERS — ✓ Basil, Onions — ⊘ Beans

SUMMER SQUASH — ✓ Beans, Corn, Garden peas, Radishes — ⊘ Potatoes

ZUCCHINI / TOMATOES — ✓ Basil, Carrots, Cucumbers, Squash (as a part of a three-way companionship) — ⊘ Cole crops, Corn, Potatoes

✓ **Companion plants**   ⊘ **Plants to Avoid**

A tried, tested, and true gardening method is companion planting, which involves growing diverse plants next to one another for mutual benefit. This method relies on interactions that naturally occur between plants to create a more balanced garden ecosystem. Strategic pairing of plants improves their growth, enhance flavor, deter pest, attracts beneficial insects and even boost soil fertility.

. For example, planting marigolds alongside tomatoes can help repel nematodes, which are harmful to tomato roots, while basil not only enhances the flavor of tomatoes but also helps to ward off aphids and tomato hornworms. The idea is that certain plants have natural affinities that, when placed together, can lead to a healthier, more resilient garden.

Natural control of pests is one of companion planting's main advantages. Certain plants release compounds or fragrances that discourage pest insects, while other plants draw beneficial insects that feed on the pests. This helps keep the garden in a more naturally regulated state and lessens the need for artificial pesticides. For instance, nasturtiums are often planted near beans or squash because they attract aphids away from these crops, serving as a "trap crop." Another major advantage is increased productivity and development. Legumes are among the plants that fix nitrogen in the soil, nourishing it for nearby plants like leafy greens and corn that need more nitrogen. Higher yields are the result of this symbiotic connection, which also improves plant health.

While scientific evidence is largely anecdotal, many gardeners swear by the practice that the flavor of their crops were improved due to companion planting. For example, planting garlic or onions near carrots is believed to enhance the sweetness of the carrots while also repelling pests like carrot flies. Companion planting also has the ability to draw pollinators and beneficial insects, both of which are necessary for the fruiting plants' ability to reproduce. Flowers like sunflowers, borage, and zinnias attract bees and butterflies, while herbs like dill and fennel attract predatory insects like ladybugs and lacewings, which feed on garden pests.

Weed suppression is another benefit of companion planting. Certain plants act as natural ground cover, shading the soil and suffocating weeds. For example, the large leaves of squash and pumpkins cover the ground, reducing the need for manual weeding. Comfrey and dandelions are deep-rooted plants that help plants whose roots do not run deep into the soil by bringing up and making available nutrients present in the deep layers of the soil. Legumes, on the other hand, are nitrogen fixation plants, helping other plants by making nitrogen available in the soil.

Companion planting makes better use of the available area in the garden. For instance, growing lettuce or spinach under taller plants like tomatoes or corn takes advantage of the shade provided by the taller plants, extending the growing season for cool-season crops. Trellises can be used to cultivate climbing plants, such as beans, freeing up ground area for other crops. Companion planting can help prevent the spread of diseases in the garden. There is a lesser chance of disease outbreak with improved air circulation and barrier creation. For example, planting onions or garlic between rows of other crops can create a natural barrier against fungal diseases. Additionally, planting a diverse mix of crops can reduce the risk of disease by avoiding the pitfalls of monoculture, where a single disease can devastate an entire crop.

CROP ROTATION AND POLYCULTURES

CROP ROTATION

Crop rotation is a fundamental practice in sustainable gardening and agriculture that involves the systematic alternation of different types of crops in a specific sequence across a particular piece of land over multiple growing seasons.

This technique is not just about planting different crops year after year; it's about strategically planning the sequence of crops to maximize soil health, manage pests and diseases, and optimize crop yields.

Many pests and pathogens are crop-specific, meaning they thrive when their preferred host is consistently available. Rotating crops allows gardeners disrupt these cycles, reducing the overall pest population and disease pressure. For instance, if a garden bed is used to grow tomatoes, which are susceptible to a variety of soil-borne diseases, planting a different crop like beans in that spot the following year can help prevent the buildup of those pathogens in the soil.

Beyond pest and disease management, crop rotation also maintains and improves soil fertility. Different crops have varying nutrient needs and rooting depths, and by rotating them, gardeners can more effectively manage soil nutrients. Furthermore, since they have a symbiotic association with nitrogen-fixing bacteria that allows them to fix atmospheric nitrogen in the soil, legumes like peas and beans are very important in a rotation plan. This process naturally enriches the soil with nitrogen, benefiting the crops that follow, especially those with high nitrogen demands like leafy greens.

There are several common methods and patterns of crop rotation, often based on the types of plants being grown. One popular method is the four-year rotation cycle, which divides crops into categories such as legumes, leafy greens, root vegetables, and fruiting vegetables. In this system, the rotation might look something like this: Year 1: Legumes (beans, peas), Year 2: Leafy Greens (lettuce, spinach), Year 3: Root Vegetables (carrots, beets), Year 4: Fruiting Vegetables (tomatoes, peppers). This cycle ensures that each type of crop is grown in a different bed each year, preventing the buildup of specific pests and nutrient depletion associated with any one type of plant.

In addition to this basic cycle, more complex rotations can be designed depending on the specific crops being grown and the gardener's goals. For instance, in larger gardens or farms, a more elaborate rotation might include cover crops like clover or buckwheat, which are planted to rest and rejuvenate the soil between cash crops. These cover crops can help prevent erosion, add organic matter, and fix nitrogen, further enhancing soil health.

When planning a crop rotation, consider certain characteristics of what you want to plant. Some plants, like brassicas (e.g., cabbage, broccoli, kale), are heavy feeders that deplete the soil of nutrients, particularly nitrogen. After growing brassicas, it's beneficial to follow with a crop that can help replenish the soil, such as legumes. Similarly, root crops like potatoes or carrots can be followed by leafy greens or other crops with shallower root systems, to take advantage of the different layers of soil.

While crop rotation is highly beneficial, it is important to plan and also keep records of the process. Knowing what was planted and where it was planted is important to ensure that the rotation is effective. Many gardeners find it helpful to create a garden map or use a garden planner to track their crop rotation over multiple seasons.

POLYCULTURE

	CHARD
	BEAN
	RADISH

Polyculture is a diverse and sustainable approach to gardening and farming that involves cultivating many crops in one area. In contrast to monoculture, which involves planting a single crop across a wide region, polyculture grows a range of plants that mutually benefit one another in an effort to replicate the diversity seen in natural ecosystems. This method increases biodiversity and also enhances the resilience of the garden or farm, leading to a range of benefits such as improved soil health, pest and disease control, efficient use of resources, and greater yields.

Polyculture creates more resilient and balanced ecosystem and this ability is one of it's many usefulness. When different species are grown together, it reduces the vulnerability of crops to pests and diseases. In a monoculture system, a pest outbreak can quickly spread and devastate an entire crop because there's no diversity to slow its progress. In contrast, a polyculture system can naturally limit pest populations because the presence of multiple plant species creates a more complex environment that's harder for pests to navigate. Additionally, some plants in a polyculture can act as natural repellents for pests, protecting more vulnerable crops. Marigolds, for instance, can help ward off worms and aphids when planted alongside vegetables, while herbs like mint and basil can keep flies and mosquitoes away. However, mint, unlike basil, is highly invasive. If you don't want mint spreading uncontrollably, it should be planted in containers or otherwise contained to prevent it from taking over the garden.

Polyculture also promotes soil health and fertility by supporting a more dynamic and sustainable use of nutrients. Different plants have distinct nutritional needs and root systems, which means they can access different layers of the soil and utilize resources more efficiently. For instance, deep-rooted plants like carrots or parsnips can draw nutrients from deeper in the soil, while shallow-rooted plants like lettuce or spinach can absorb nutrients from the surface layers. This complementary use of resources helps prevent nutrient depletion and lessens the use for artificial fertilizers.

Water management is another area where polyculture shines. The diversity of plants in a polyculture system means that water is used more efficiently, as different plants may have different water needs and can occupy different niches within the soil. For example, the deep roots of certain crops can help draw moisture up from deeper soil layers, while the dense foliage of other plants can shade the soil and reduce evaporation, conserving water. Additionally, polyculture systems often include ground cover plants that protect the soil from erosion and help retain moisture. Because of this, polyculture is especially well adapted for areas with scarce water supplies or erratic rainfall patterns.

Polyculture also fosters greater biodiversity, not just among plants but also within the wider ecosystem. Many beneficial insects, birds, and other wildlife can be drawn to a wide range of crops, which can assist in pollinating plants and decreasing pest populations. Pollinators like bees and butterflies are more likely to visit a garden that offers a range of flowers and habitats, leading to better pollination and higher fruit and seed yields. Predatory insects like ladybugs and lacewings, which feed on pests like aphids, are also more likely to thrive in a polyculture environment where they can find a steady supply of food and shelter. A healthier garden and a more resilient ecosystem result from the use of fewer chemical pesticides due to this natural insect management.

Native American tribes' "Three Sisters" method—growing maize, beans, and squash together—is one of the most well-known instances of polyculture. In this arrangement, the squash spreads throughout the ground, keeping moisture and controlling weeds, the beans add nitrogen to the soil, and the corn acts as a natural trellis for the beans to climb. This interdependent relationship allows each crop to thrive while supporting the others, demonstrating the power of polyculture to create a self-sustaining system.

Polyculture is also highly adaptable and can be implemented in various garden sizes and types. In small gardens, companion planting—a form of polyculture where specific plants are paired together for mutual benefit—is a common practice. For example, planting tomatoes with basil not only enhances the flavor of the tomatoes but also helps repel pests. In larger gardens or farms, more complex polycultures can be designed to include a wide range of crops, trees, and even animals, creating a dynamic and resilient agricultural system.

In urban settings, polyculture can be applied through practices like vertical gardening, container gardening, and rooftop gardens, where multiple types of plants are grown together in limited spaces. These urban polycultures can lower the urban heat island effect, increase local food security, and supply fresh vegetables.

While polyculture offers numerous benefits, it does require careful planning and management. Understanding the relationships between different plants, including their growth habits, nutrient needs, and pest interactions, is crucial to creating a successful polyculture system. Gardeners and farmers must consider factors such as plant spacing, timing, and succession planting to ensure that all crops have the resources they need to thrive. Also, polyculture systems can be more labor-intensive, especially in the initial stages, as they require careful observation and adaptation to maintain balance and productivity, but the reward justifies the labor.

CHAPTER

8

STARTING FROM SEED

Seed planting in a survival garden is a fundamental aspect of creating a self-sustaining food source that can thrive even under challenging conditions. This practice is crucial for those who want to ensure a steady supply of fresh, nutritious produce while also being prepared for situations where traditional supply chains might be disrupted. In a survival garden, the process of seed planting goes beyond mere cultivation; it involves careful planning, selection, and management to optimize food production and resilience.

SEED SELECTION AND STORAGE

Seed selection and storage are crucial elements of successful gardening, especially in the context of survival gardening where self-sufficiency and sustainability are key priorities. Selecting the right seeds is fundamental for a productive garden. Would your local climate condition be good for the seeds you want to select?

Certain factors are to be put into considerations when selecting seeds. Plants that are suited to your specific weather conditions and soil type will be more resilient and productive. For example, if you live in a region with hot summers, opting for heat-tolerant varieties like okra or drought-resistant tomatoes can lead to better outcomes. Conversely, in cooler climates, cold-hardy crops such as kale and peas are more likely to thrive. Additionally, deciding between heirloom and hybrid seeds is crucial. Open-pollinated heirloom seeds are passed down through the generations and often offer rich flavors and the ability to save seeds for future planting. Hybrid seeds, created by cross-pollinating different plant varieties, can provide specific benefits such as disease resistance or higher yields, but they may not produce seeds with the same traits as the parent plants; it's also possible that the seeds do not germinate at all, making them an inconvenient option except in specific cases.

Another important consideration is disease resistance. Selecting seeds that are resistant to common pests and diseases can significantly improve the health and yield of your crops. For instance, choosing blight-resistant tomato varieties can help avoid crop loss due to disease. Seed purity and viability are also essential; high-quality seeds with a high germination rate are more likely to produce healthy plants. Purchasing seeds from reputable sources ensures you're getting viable seeds. Crop diversity should not be overlooked; growing a variety of crops ensures a balanced diet and enhances garden resilience. Different plants can provide various nutrients and support each other in the garden ecosystem, improving overall productivity.

Once you've selected the right seeds, you will need to adapt appropriate storage methods to preserve them for later use. Seeds can lose their capacity to germinate if not stored properly. Seeds should be kept in a dry environment to prevent premature germination and mold. Before storing, make sure seeds are thoroughly dry and then place them in airtight containers. Tight-fitted glass jars or moisture-proof envelopes are ideal. The temperature of the environment matters and affects the storage capacity of the seed. Seeds should be stored ideally between 32°F and 50°F. If seeds are stored in sealed containers to prevent humidity, a refrigerator might be a great alternative for storing them, but take care not to store the seeds with other fruits, flowers, or vegetables: the ethylene gas produced during ripening may cause stunted germination rates or make the seeds unqualified for growth. Another necessary condition is darkness; seeds should be kept in a dark environment to stop light from causing germination. Proper labeling and organization help keep track of seed types, varieties, and storage dates, ensuring you use the oldest seeds first and plan your garden efficiently.

For long-term storage, especially in a survival gardening context, freezing seeds can extend their shelf life. However, if the seeds are not extremely dried, freezing may damage them. Properly dried and stored seeds can last several years in the freezer, which is particularly useful for preserving heirloom or rare varieties. Additionally, seed saving is a valuable practice for self-sufficiency. Harvesting and storing seeds from your own plants can maintain a continuous seed supply and adapt plants to your specific growing conditions over time. Effective seed saving involves choosing healthy plants, understanding cross-pollination risks, and using proper drying and storage techniques.

SEED STARTING TECHNIQUES

Starting seeds is a fundamental aspect of gardening, crucial for anyone aiming to grow a thriving garden, whether for survival or simply for pleasure. This process starts by choosing the right containers. Containers need to provide enough space for the developing seedlings and include proper drainage to prevent waterlogging. Seed trays, peat pots, and biodegradable pots are common choices, each offering benefits for different gardening situations. Seed trays are efficient for starting multiple seeds in a small space, while peat and biodegradable pots are advantageous because they can be planted directly into the ground, reducing transplant shock.

The medium in which you start your seeds is equally important. A light weight, well-drained and sterile environment is a better seed starting mix than just opting for garden soil. Components found in seed starting mixes like perlite, peat moss and vermiculite help keep moisture and allow aeration to the roots thereby helping seed germination. Another significant consideration is timing; seedlings benefit from an early start when seeds are started inside several weeks prior to the latest day of frost in where you live. For most seeds to sprout, a warm temperature is needed, usually between 65°F and 75°F (18°C and 24°C). Consistent temperature maintenance may allow for quicker and more even germination of seedlings when a seedling heat pad is used.

Light is vital for seedlings to develop well. Once seeds have germinated, enough light is needed for healthy growth. Indoor gardeners should use grow lights or fluorescent lights designed for seed starting, positioning them close to the seedlings and providing 12 to 16 hours of light daily to simulate natural sunlight. Outdoor gardeners should ensure their seeds receive adequate sunlight by placing containers in sunny locations or using cold frames to shield seedlings from harsh weather.

When it comes to planting seeds, adhere to the depth and spacing recommendations listed on the seed packs. In general, seeds need to be sown around twice as deep as their size. Small seeds are encouraged to germinate by being gently pressed into the soil's surface and covered with a thin coating of seed starting mix, which also helps to retain moisture. Water sparingly so as not to disturb the seeds; the soil should be evenly damp but not soggy. Using a fine mist spray bottle or bottom watering methods helps prevent the soil from becoming too soggy.

Once seedlings emerge, thinning them is essential to prevent overcrowding, which can lead to weak growth and competition for resources. Thin seedlings by snipping the weaker ones at soil level, leaving the strongest to grow. This practice ensures each plant has enough space and reduces the risk of diseases by improving airflow. When seedlings reach a manageable size and have sprouted their first true leaves, they can be transplanted into bigger pots or planted straight into the garden. Harden off seedlings over many days to reduce transplant shock and gradually accustom them to outside environments.

Maintaining seedling health involves regular monitoring for pests, diseases, and nutrient deficiencies. Adequate light, water, and airflow are necessary for strong growth. A gentle fan can enhance air circulation and strengthen seedlings, while consistent warmth supports optimal development. For those new to gardening or seeking convenience, seed starting kits are an excellent option. These kits typically include containers, seed starting mix, and sometimes seeds, making the process more straightforward and manageable.

TRANSPLANTING SEEDLINGS

Transplanting seedlings is a pivotal stage in gardening, marking the transition from initial growth in small containers to their new homes, whether in larger pots or directly in the garden. This process is essential for their continued development and success. Timing is key; when a seedling develops its first set of genuine leaves and a robust root system, it's usually time to transplant it. The best time for transplanting is around 4 to 6 weeks after sowing, though this can vary by plant type. Before moving them, ensure that the new planting area or containers are well-prepared.

This entails aerating the soil in garden beds and adding organic materials, such as compost. Select pots for your containers that have sufficient drainage, then fill them with premium potting mix. Once again, these pots must be sterilized using bleach and then drying in the sun before use to eliminate possible bacterial or fungal infection. Hardening off is the process of acclimating seedlings to their new surroundings before to transplanting. This slow, steady exposure lessens stress and aids in the seedlings' adaptation to the outer environment. Start by putting seedlings in a shady, protected area for a few hours every day. Over the course of seven to ten days, gradually increase the amount of sunshine and outside temperature that the seedlings get. Once the seedlings are ready, handle them with care to avoid damaging their fragile roots and stems. Gently remove them from their containers, supporting the root ball to prevent breakage. Planting bio-degradable pots can be done in a bigger container or directly in the ground.

Dig holes that are just a little bit bigger than the root balls when planting seedlings in garden beds, being sure to space them out according to the guidelines specific to each type of plant. With the top of the root ball level with the soil's surface, plant each seedling in the hole at the same depth as it was growing in the container. To remove any air pockets, carefully press the dirt into the hole and cover the roots. Give the newly planted roots plenty of water to help the soil settle and stay wet.

When choosing pots for container planting, make sure the pots are at least 2 inches bigger in diameter than the one they are already in. Create a hole in the middle of the container, set the seedling inside, and then cover the hole with potting mix. To make sure the dirt has excellent contact with the roots, gently press it down; do not pack it down too firmly, though. Another technique to ensure the soil has contact with the roots is to remove air pockets by gently tapping the bottom of the pot on a flat surface, which causes air to rise to the surface and dissipate. This can be done both before and after planting. After planting, give the soil plenty of water to help the seedlings take root. Watering will also help remove air bubbles, which can be observed as bubbles rise to the surface as the water is absorbed

The seedlings need extra attention after transplantation so they can get used to their new surroundings. Keep them away from intense sunshine and wind, since these can harm immature plants. Mulch applied around the base might aid in controlling soil temperature and moisture retention. It's critical to water the soil often to maintain a constant, slightly damp texture. Keep an eye out for symptoms of transplant shock, such yellowing or withering leaves, and take quick action to resolve any problems. After the seedlings have taken root, begin fertilizing them in accordance with the requirements of each individual plant. To prevent overfertilization, use a water-soluble fertilizer that is balanced and apply it according to the specified rates. To guarantee the seedlings' healthy growth, keep an eye out for illnesses and pests and take swift action when necessary.

CHAPTER 9

VEGETABLE GARDENING

Vegetable gardening is an enriching and practical endeavor that brings numerous benefits. Vegetable gardening involves cultivating edible plants for consumption, and it can be adapted to suit a variety of spaces, from sprawling backyard plots to compact urban balconies. Vegetables grown in your garden can be harvested at their peak ripeness, offering superior flavor and a higher nutritional value compared to those picked early and transported long distances.

Consider factors such as your local growing season, average temperatures, and soil conditions before planting. For instance, spinach and lettuce thrive in the spring and fall, while peppers and tomatoes need the heat of summer to flourish.

Regardless of the method, proper soil preparation is key to a successful vegetable garden. Good soil should be rich in organic matter, well-draining, and capable of holding moisture while allowing roots to access nutrients.

For veggies to develop well, it's important to plant them in the proper circumstances and at the right time. Take into account variables like temperature swings and frost dates in addition to adhering to the prescribed planting dates for each kind of crop. Using a gardening calendar specific to your area may be quite beneficial since planting too early or too late will influence your produce. To guarantee that every plant has adequate space to thrive without fighting for resources, proper spacing is also crucial.

Taking care of and watering your vegetable garden is a continuous process that demands focus.

Consistent moisture is essential for healthy plant development, but overwatering can lead to root rot and other issues. Mulching the area surrounding your plants may help control temperature, keep the soil wet, and lessen weed growth. A plentiful crop may also be guaranteed by routinely pulling weeds and keeping an eye out for pests and illnesses.

You might need to give some of the plants assistance as your veggies develop. For instance, stakes or cages are frequently needed to hold cucumbers and tomatoes upright and avoid sprawling. Timely harvesting and proper maintenance are also essential. Vegetables have the most flavor and nutritional value when harvested when they are at peak maturity (check for firmness) just before they get overripe (will be mushy).

ROOT VEGETABLES: CARROTS, BEETS, POTATOES

Root vegetables such as carrots, beets, and potatoes are staples in many gardens, prized for their versatility, storage potential, and nutritional value. Each type of root vegetable has its own unique growing requirements and benefits, making them valuable additions to a survival garden or any home garden.

CARROTS

Carrots are renowned for their crisp texture and sweet flavor. They thrive in cool weather and can be grown in a variety of soil types, though they perform best in loose, well-drained soil free of large rocks or debris, which can cause the roots to deform. Carrots are typically direct-seeded into the garden, as they do not transplant well. The seeds are very tiny, so they should be sown thinly and covered lightly with soil. Carrots require consistent moisture for proper root development, so regular watering is essential. They also benefit from a layer of mulch to keep the soil moist and to prevent weeds from competing for nutrients. Carrots are usually ready to harvest in 70 to 80 days, depending on the variety. They can be harvested at different sizes, from baby carrots to full-sized roots, and they store well in cool, dark conditions.

BEETS

Beets are another excellent root vegetable, known for their earthy flavor and vibrant color. They are quite hardy and can be grown in a range of climates, though they prefer cooler temperatures. Beets are often started from seeds directly sown in the garden. The seeds are clusters of several seeds, so thinning is necessary to ensure proper spacing between plants, which allows the roots to grow to their full size. Beets need well-drained, fertile soil and consistent moisture to develop their round, sweet roots. Like carrots, they benefit from mulching to maintain soil moisture and control weeds. Beets typically mature in 50 to 70 days, and both the roots and the leafy greens are edible. The greens can be harvested earlier for a nutritious addition to salads, while the roots are usually left in the ground until they reach the desired size. Beets can be stored for several months in a cool, dark place.

POTATOES

Potatoes are a versatile and filling staple, ideal for various culinary applications. They are grown from seed potatoes, which are small tubers or pieces of tubers that have sprouted eyes. Potatoes require well-drained, loose soil to accommodate their growth and to prevent diseases such as rot. They are typically planted in rows, with seed potatoes placed about 4 inches deep and spaced 12 inches apart. As the plants grow, they benefit from being hilled, which involves piling soil around the base of the plants to support the developing tubers and to protect them from sunlight, which can turn them green and inedible. Potatoes need consistent moisture, especially during tuber formation. They are usually ready for harvest in 70 to 100 days, depending on the variety. Potatoes should be harvested when the plants start to die back. After harvesting, they need to be cured in a dark, well-ventilated area for a couple of weeks to toughen their skins and improve storage life. Properly cured and stored potatoes can last for several months.

Each of these root vegetables adds significant nutritional value to your diet.

Carrots are rich in beta-carotene and vitamin A, which are important for vision and immune function. Beets are high in antioxidants, fiber, and vitamins, which support overall health and digestive function. Potatoes provide essential carbohydrates, vitamins, and minerals, making them a vital part of a balanced diet.

LEAFY GREENS: SPINACH, KALE, LETTUCE

Leafy greens like spinach, kale, and lettuce are essential components of any garden, offering not only a wealth of nutrients but also versatility in the kitchen. Each of these greens has its own growing requirements and benefits, making them valuable additions to both traditional and survival gardens.

SPINACH

Spinach is a nutrient-dense leafy green known for its high content of vitamins A, C, and K, as well as iron and folate. It thrives in cooler weather and can be grown in early spring or late fall, which helps avoid the heat that can cause the plant to bolt or go to seed prematurely. Spinach prefers well-drained, fertile soil with a pH between 6.0 and 7.0. It is usually direct-seeded into the garden, as the seeds germinate best in cool soil temperatures, around 45°F to 75°F (7°C to 24°C). Spinach requires consistent moisture, so regular watering is essential to maintain the quality and size of the leaves. It can be harvested when the leaves are young and tender, usually about 40 to 50 days after planting, or when they reach a more mature size. Frequent harvesting of the outer leaves encourages continuous growth and extends the harvest period. Spinach is best used fresh but can also be blanched and frozen for later use.

KALE

Kale is a hardy leafy green that is highly valued for its robust flavor and nutritional benefits. It is rich in vitamins A, C, and K, as well as calcium and antioxidants. Kale is quite versatile and can tolerate a range of temperatures, making it suitable for both cool and mild climates. It is typically started from seeds, which can be sown directly into the garden or started indoors and then transplanted. Kale prefers well-drained, nutrient-rich soil with a pH between 6.0 and 7.0. The plant can be grown throughout the year in many regions, with cooler temperatures often enhancing its flavor. Kale grows best in full sun but can tolerate partial shade, particularly in hotter climates. It is usually ready for harvest in 55 to 75 days, depending on the variety and growing conditions. Harvesting individual leaves from the bottom of the plant allows it to continue producing new leaves from the center. Kale can be used in a variety of dishes, from salads to soups, and can be preserved by freezing or dehydrating.

LETTUCE

Lettuce is a popular leafy green that is known for its crisp texture and mild flavor. It comes in various types, including romaine, butterhead, and leaf lettuce, each with its own characteristics. Lettuce prefers cooler temperatures and can be grown in early spring and fall. It requires well-drained soil rich in organic matter and a pH level between 6.0 and 7.0. Lettuce seeds are usually sown directly into the garden, as they germinate best in cooler soil temperatures, around 40°F to 70°F (4°C to 21°C). Regular watering is important to keep the soil consistently moist and to prevent bitterness in the leaves. Lettuce can be harvested as baby greens, about 30 days after planting, or allowed to mature to full size, usually in 50 to 70 days. Harvesting individual leaves from the outer part of the plant allows it to continue producing new leaves. Lettuce is best used fresh in salads and sandwiches but can also be preserved by freezing, though this can affect its texture.

Spinach, kale, and lettuce are all relatively easy to grow and can be tailored to fit various climates and growing conditions.

FRUITING VEGETABLES: TOMATOES, PEPPERS, SQUASH

Fruiting vegetables like tomatoes, peppers, and squash are essential components of many gardens due to their versatility, rich flavors, and nutritional benefits. These plants produce fruits that are delicious and packed with vitamins and minerals. Each type of fruiting vegetable has its own specific growing requirements and benefits, making them valuable additions to a garden, whether you're cultivating a traditional backyard plot or a survival garden.

TOMATOES

Tomatoes are a favorite among gardeners for their juicy, flavorful fruits that come in a variety of sizes and colors, from the small, sweet cherry tomatoes to large, meaty beefsteaks. They thrive in warm weather and require a long growing season with plenty of sunlight. Tomatoes are typically started from seeds indoors 6-8 weeks before the last expected frost date, or they can be purchased as transplants from garden centers. When planting tomatoes in the garden, they need well-drained, fertile soil enriched with organic matter and a pH between 6.2 and 6.8. Space the plants about 18-24 inches apart to allow for their sprawling growth.

There is a stark difference between determinate and indeterminate tomato varieties when deciding on support. Indeterminate tomatoes grow and produce fruit continuously throughout the season, requiring staking or caging to support their ongoing growth and to maximize yield. These varieties benefit from regular pruning and can grow quite tall. In contrast, determinate tomatoes grow to a set height, produce fruit all at once, and then stop. While they can be supported for additional stability, they don't necessarily need staking, as their shorter, bushier growth habit is more self-supporting. This predictable growth pattern is why they are referred to as "determinate."

Assuming you're growing the indeterminate variety for year-round yield, supporting the tomato plants with stakes, cages, or trellises becomes essential to keep the fruit off the ground and to improve air circulation, which helps prevent diseases. Tomatoes also need consistent watering and should be kept evenly moist, as fluctuations in soil moisture can lead to issues like blossom end rot. They typically begin producing fruit 60-85 days after planting, depending on the variety. Regular harvesting of ripe tomatoes encourages the plant to produce more fruit throughout the growing season. Tomatoes are highly versatile in the kitchen, used fresh in salads, cooked into sauces, or preserved through canning.

PEPPERS

Peppers are another popular fruiting vegetable, known for their vibrant colors and diverse flavors, ranging from sweet bell peppers to hot chili peppers. Like tomatoes, peppers thrive in warm conditions and require a long growing season. Start pepper seeds indoors 8-10 weeks before the last frost date or purchase seedlings from a nursery. Peppers need well-drained, fertile soil with a pH between 6.0 and 7.0. When planting, space the plants about 18-24 inches apart to allow for their growth and to ensure adequate air circulation. Peppers benefit from consistent watering and may require additional support as they grow, particularly for larger varieties. They are sensitive to cold and should be planted outdoors only after all danger of frost has passed and the soil has warmed. Peppers typically start producing fruit 70-90 days after planting. Harvesting peppers can be done at various stages, depending on the desired flavor and color. Sweet peppers are often harvested when fully colored, while hot peppers can be picked at any stage, from green to red, depending on the heat level desired. Peppers can be enjoyed fresh, cooked, or preserved through freezing or drying.

SQUASH

Squash encompasses a wide range of varieties, including summer squash (like zucchini) and winter squash (such as butternut and acorn squash). Summer squash is known for its tender, edible skin and mild flavor, while winter squash has a tougher skin and is typically harvested when fully mature for long-term storage. Squash plants are typically direct-seeded into the garden or started indoors and then transplanted. They require warm soil temperatures and a long growing season, with summer squash generally maturing in 50-70 days and winter squash in 80-100 days. Squash plants need well-drained, fertile soil with a pH between 6.0 and 7.5. Space the plants adequately to accommodate their sprawling growth—about 36-48 inches apart for most varieties. Consistent watering is crucial for squash, particularly during fruit development, to ensure optimal growth and to prevent issues like blossom end rot. Summer squash should be harvested when the fruits are young and tender, while winter squash should be left on the vine until the skin is hard and the plant starts to die back. Both types of squash can be used in a variety of dishes, from stir-fries and casseroles to soups and pies.

CHAPTER 10

FRUIT AND NUT TREES

SELECTING AND PLANTING FRUIT TREES

Selecting and planting fruit trees is a rewarding endeavor that can transform your garden into a productive and beautiful landscape. The process involves careful consideration of several factors, including the type of fruit tree, the local climate, soil conditions, and the tree's specific needs. Proper planning and execution in selecting and planting fruit trees can lead to years of bountiful harvests and enhanced garden enjoyment.

CHOOSING THE RIGHT FRUIT TREES

When selecting fruit trees for your garden, it's important to start with a clear understanding of your local climate and soil conditions. Different fruit trees thrive in different environments, so choosing varieties suited to your region is crucial. For example, apple trees generally require a cold winter period to produce fruit, making them ideal for cooler climates, whereas citrus trees need warmer temperatures and might struggle in colder areas. Researching local recommendations and talking to local nurseries or extension services can provide valuable insights into which varieties are best suited for your area.

Beyond climate compatibility, consider the space available in your garden. Some fruit trees, like standard apple or pear trees, can grow quite large and require ample space for their canopy and root system. If you have limited space, dwarf or semi-dwarf varieties might be a better choice. These trees are smaller but still produce a good amount of fruit. Additionally, think about how the tree will fit into your garden design. Fruit trees can serve as focal points, provide shade, or even act as hedges, so their placement should enhance both their aesthetic appeal and functional role in your garden.

PREPARING FOR PLANTING

Once you've selected the right fruit trees, the next step is to prepare your garden for planting. Good soil preparation is essential for healthy tree growth. Fruit trees generally prefer well-drained soil rich in organic matter. Conduct a soil test to determine your soil's pH and nutrient levels. Most fruit trees thrive in soil with a pH between 6.0 and 7.0. If your soil is too acidic or alkaline, you might need to amend it with lime or sulfur to adjust the pH. Incorporating compost or well-rotted manure can improve soil fertility and structure, helping the tree's roots establish more effectively.

The planting site should receive adequate sunlight, as most fruit trees require full sun to produce fruit. Aim for a location that gets at least six to eight hours of direct sunlight each day. Avoid planting in low-lying areas where water tends to collect, as this can lead to root rot. Ensure the site is sheltered from strong winds, which can damage young trees and hinder their growth.

PLANTING FRUIT TREES

The actual planting process is a critical phase that sets the stage for your tree's future health and productivity. Begin by digging a hole that is twice as wide and the same depth as the root ball of the tree. This allows the roots to spread out and establish themselves more easily. If you're planting more than one tree, make sure to space them appropriately to allow for their mature size. For most standard-sized fruit trees, this means spacing them at least 15 to 20 feet apart.

Before planting, inspect the roots of the tree. If they are circling the root ball or appear densely packed, gently tease them apart or make a few vertical cuts to encourage outward growth. Place the tree in the center of the hole, ensuring that the graft union (the point where the rootstock and scion meet) is at or slightly above ground level. This is crucial for the tree's long-term health, as planting too deep can cause the tree to struggle and reduce its lifespan.

Backfill the hole with the excavated soil, gently tamping it down to remove air pockets. Water the tree thoroughly after planting to help settle the soil and ensure good root-to-soil contact. Applying a layer of mulch around the base of the tree helps retain moisture, suppress weeds, and regulate soil temperature. However, avoid piling mulch against the trunk, as this can lead to rot.

CARING FOR YOUNG FRUIT TREES

After planting, young fruit trees require ongoing care to help them establish and grow. Watering is critical, especially during the first few years. Fruit trees need consistent moisture, but overwatering can be as detrimental as underwatering. Aim to keep the soil evenly moist, but not soggy. A deep watering once a week is often sufficient, but adjust based on rainfall and soil conditions.

Fertilizing your fruit trees will support their growth and fruit production. Use a balanced fertilizer or one specifically formulated for fruit trees, following the manufacturer's instructions. Avoid fertilizing too early in the season, as this can encourage excessive leaf growth at the expense of fruit development. Typically, a spring application and possibly a mid-summer application are sufficient.

Pruning is another essential aspect of fruit tree care. Proper pruning helps shape the tree, remove dead or diseased wood, and improve air circulation. It also encourages the development of a strong framework for fruit production. Most fruit trees benefit from a yearly pruning session, preferably in late winter or early spring before new growth begins. The specific pruning techniques will vary depending on the type of fruit tree and its growth habits.

PEST AND DISEASE MANAGEMENT

Fruit trees are susceptible to various pests and diseases, so monitoring and management are crucial. Common pests include aphids, spider mites, and fruit flies, while diseases can range from fungal infections like powdery mildew to bacterial issues like fire blight. Regularly inspect your trees for signs of trouble, such as discolored leaves, wilting, or unusual spots on the fruit.

Integrated pest management (IPM) strategies can help control pests and diseases. This approach combines cultural practices, biological controls, and, if necessary, chemical treatments. For example, introducing beneficial insects like ladybugs can help control aphid populations, while proper spacing and pruning improve air circulation and reduce disease risk. If chemical treatments are needed, always follow label instructions and consider organic options to minimize environmental impact.

HARVESTING AND ENJOYING YOUR FRUIT

As your fruit trees mature, you'll eventually enjoy the fruits of your labor. Harvesting times will vary depending on the type of fruit tree and the variety. Generally, fruit is ready to harvest when it has reached its full color and firmness, and often, a slight give when gently squeezed. For example, apples should be harvested when they come off the tree easily, while peaches should be picked when they are slightly soft to the touch.

Proper harvesting techniques are important to avoid damaging the fruit or the tree. Use clean, sharp pruners or scissors to cut the fruit from the tree, leaving a small portion of the stem attached. Handle the fruit gently to prevent bruising and store it in a cool, dry place until you're ready to enjoy it. Many fruits, like apples and pears, can be stored for several weeks or even months under the right conditions, allowing you to enjoy your harvest long after picking.

NUT TREES FOR LONG-TERM SUSTAINABILITY

Nut trees are a fantastic choice for any garden focused on long-term sustainability. These trees not only provide a rich source of nutrients and healthy fats but also contribute to the ecological balance of your garden or landscape. With proper selection, planting, and care, nut trees can become a staple in your self-sufficient garden, offering both economic and environmental benefits.

CHOOSING NUT TREES

When selecting nut trees for your garden, it's important to consider the climate, soil conditions, and the specific needs of each tree. Different nut trees have varying requirements and characteristics, so choosing varieties that are well-suited to your local environment will ensure better growth and productivity.

- **Almonds:** Almond trees thrive in warm climates with well-drained soil and a good amount of sunlight. They require a chilling period of about 600-1,000 hours of temperatures below 45°F (7°C) to produce fruit, making them suitable for regions with cold winters. Almond trees need space to spread their branches and can grow quite large, so ensure you have enough room for their mature size.

- **Walnuts:**Walnuts are adaptable to various climates but prefer well-drained soil and full sun. They can be sensitive to extreme cold, so choose varieties that are suited to your region's winter conditions. Walnuts are large trees and require ample space for their roots and canopy. They also produce a significant amount of leaf litter, which can be composted or used as mulch.

- **Pecans:**Pecans are ideal for warmer climates and are well-suited to areas with long growing seasons. They need a good amount of water and well-drained soil to thrive. Pecans also have specific pollination requirements, so it's important to plant compatible varieties nearby to ensure successful nut production.

- **Hazelnuts**: Hazelnut trees are more tolerant of cooler climates and can be a good option for regions with moderate winters. They prefer well-drained soil and full sun but can also tolerate partial shade. Hazelnuts are generally smaller trees, making them suitable for smaller spaces or urban gardens.

PREPARING FOR PLANTING

Proper preparation is key to establishing healthy nut trees that will thrive for years. Start by choosing a suitable planting site that meets the specific needs of the nut tree varieties you've selected. Most nut trees require well-drained soil and full sun, though some can tolerate partial shade. Conduct a soil test to determine the pH and nutrient levels, and amend the soil as needed to meet the needs of your chosen trees. Most nut trees prefer a soil pH between 6.0 and 7.0.

Before planting, it's important to select healthy, disease-free nursery stock. Look for trees with well-developed root systems and a sturdy trunk. Avoid trees with signs of damage, disease, or poor growth. If you're planting bare-root trees, soak the roots in water for a few hours before planting to help them recover from transplanting stress.

PLANTING NUT TREES

The planting process is crucial for the long-term success of your nut trees. Begin by digging a hole that is twice as wide and as deep as the root ball of the tree. This will help the roots establish themselves more easily. Place the tree in the center of the hole, ensuring that the graft union (if applicable) is at or slightly above the soil level. Backfill the hole with the excavated soil, gently tamping it down to remove air pockets. Water the tree thoroughly after planting to help settle the soil and ensure good root-to-soil contact.

Mulch around the base of the tree helps retain soil moisture, regulate soil temperature, and suppress weeds. Apply a layer of organic mulch, such as wood chips or straw, but avoid piling it directly against the trunk to prevent rot.

CARING FOR NUT TREES

Once planted, nut trees require ongoing care to thrive and produce a bountiful harvest. Watering is essential, especially during the first few years as the tree establishes itself. Nut trees generally need deep, infrequent watering to encourage deep root growth. Avoid overwatering, as this can lead to root rot. A deep watering once a week or as needed based on weather conditions is typically sufficient.

Fertilization supports healthy growth and nut production. Use a balanced fertilizer or one specifically formulated for nut trees, following the manufacturer's instructions. Avoid over-fertilizing, which can lead to excessive vegetative growth at the expense of nut production.

Pruning is another important aspect of nut tree care. Proper pruning helps shape the tree, remove dead or diseased wood, and improve air circulation. It also encourages the development of a strong framework for fruiting. Most nut trees benefit from annual pruning, preferably in late winter or early spring before new growth begins. The specific pruning techniques will vary depending on the type of nut tree.

PEST AND DISEASE MANAGEMENT

Nut trees can be susceptible to various pests and diseases. Common pests include aphids, mites, and weevils, while diseases can range from fungal infections to bacterial issues. Regular monitoring is essential to catch any problems early. Integrated pest management (IPM) strategies can help control pests and diseases. This approach combines cultural practices, biological controls, and, if necessary, chemical treatments.

For example, introducing beneficial insects like ladybugs can help control aphid populations, while proper spacing and pruning improve air circulation and reduce disease risk. If chemical treatments are needed, always follow label instructions and consider organic options to minimize environmental impact.

HARVESTING AND STORING NUTS

Harvesting nuts at the right time is crucial for optimal flavor and quality. Most nuts are ready to harvest when the shells have hardened, and the nuts begin to fall from the tree. For example, walnuts are harvested when the outer husk starts to split, while almonds are ready when the shells become dry and brittle.

Use a gentle hand when harvesting to avoid damaging the tree or the nuts. For most nut trees, you can simply shake the branches or use a rake to gather fallen nuts from the ground. After harvesting, nuts need to be cleaned and dried before storage. Remove any remaining husks or debris and spread the nuts out in a single layer to dry in a well-ventilated area. Properly dried nuts can be stored in a cool, dry place for several months or even longer, depending on the type of nut.

LONG-TERM SUSTAINABILITY AND BENEFITS

Nut trees offer long-term sustainability benefits beyond their nutritional value. They contribute to soil health by improving soil structure and fertility through their root systems and leaf litter. Nut trees also provide habitat and food for wildlife, supporting biodiversity in your garden or landscape. They can help reduce your environmental footprint by providing a renewable source of food and reducing the need for store-bought nuts, which often come with packaging and transportation costs.

BERRY BUSHES AND VINES

Berry bushes and vines are a delightful addition to any garden, offering not only delicious fruit but also a range of benefits that make them an excellent choice for sustainable and productive gardening. These plants are relatively easy to grow, provide multiple harvests throughout the growing season, and can enhance the aesthetic appeal of your garden with their vibrant foliage and colorful berries. Understanding how to select, plant, and care for berry bushes and vines will help you create a thriving garden that yields abundant, fresh fruit.

CHOOSING BERRY BUSHES AND VINES

When selecting berry bushes and vines, consider the local climate, soil conditions, and the specific needs of each type of plant. Different berries have varying requirements and characteristics, so choosing varieties suited to your region will ensure better growth and fruit production.

- **Blueberries:** Blueberries are a popular choice for home gardeners due to their sweet, nutritious fruit and attractive foliage. They thrive in acidic soils with a pH between 4.5 and 5.5. Blueberries prefer well-drained, sandy loam soil and require full sun for optimal fruiting. When selecting blueberry varieties, consider choosing both highbush and lowbush types, as they have different harvest times and can provide a longer fruiting season.

- **Raspberries:** Raspberries are versatile and can be grown in various climates, but they generally prefer well-drained, fertile soil with a pH between 5.5 and 6.8. They come in summer-bearing and everbearing varieties. Summer-bearing raspberries produce fruit once a year, typically in early summer, while everbearing varieties can produce fruit twice a year, once in early summer and again in late summer or fall.

- **Blackberries:** Blackberries are similar to raspberries but generally have larger fruit and can be grown in a wider range of climates. They prefer well-drained soil with a pH between 5.5 and 6.5. Blackberries can be thorny or thornless, and they come in erect, trailing, and semi-erect growth habits. Thornless varieties are often preferred for easier harvesting.

- **Grapes:** Grapevines are another excellent choice for home gardens, providing fresh fruit along with the option to make homemade grape juice. Grapevines thrive in well-drained soil with a pH between 6.0 and 6.8 and require full sun. There are numerous grape varieties, so choose one that fits your growing conditions and intended use.

PREPARING FOR PLANTING

Proper preparation is key to establishing healthy berry bushes and vines. Start by choosing a suitable planting site that meets the specific needs of the plants. Most berry bushes and vines require full sun to partial shade, though some may tolerate more shade. Conduct a soil test to determine the pH and nutrient levels, and amend the soil as needed. For example, blueberries require acidic soil, so you may need to amend your soil with sulfur or peat moss to achieve the right pH.

PLANTING BERRY BUSHES AND VINES

When planting berry bushes and vines, follow these general guidelines to ensure successful establishment and growth. For most berry bushes, dig a hole that is twice as wide and as deep as the root ball. This allows the roots to spread out and establish more easily. Space plants according to their mature size to ensure adequate air circulation and prevent overcrowding. For instance, blueberry bushes should be spaced about 4-5 feet apart, while raspberry and blackberry canes should be spaced 2-3 feet apart.

When planting grapevines, dig a hole that is large enough to accommodate the root system, and plant the vine so that the graft union (where the rootstock meets the vine) is just above soil level. Grapevines generally require more space, so plant them about 6-8 feet apart, depending on the variety and the support structure you plan to use.

CARING FOR BERRY BUSHES AND VINES

After planting, berry bushes and vines require ongoing care to thrive and produce a bountiful harvest. Watering is essential, especially during the first few years as the plants establish themselves. Most berry plants need consistent moisture, but overwatering can be detrimental. Aim to keep the soil evenly moist, and adjust watering based on weather conditions and soil type.

Fertilization supports healthy growth and fruit production. Use a balanced fertilizer or one specifically formulated for the type of berry or vine you are growing. Follow the manufacturer's instructions and avoid over-fertilizing, which can lead to excessive foliage growth at the expense of fruit production.

Pruning is another important aspect of berry care. Proper pruning helps shape the plants, remove dead or diseased wood, and improve air circulation. For raspberries and blackberries, pruning involves removing old canes after they have fruited and thinning new canes to encourage healthy growth. Blueberries benefit from annual pruning to remove old, unproductive wood and to shape the bush. Grapevines require regular pruning to control their growth, improve air circulation, and promote better fruit production.

PEST AND DISEASE MANAGEMENT

Berry bushes and vines can be susceptible to various pests and diseases. Common pests include aphids, spider mites, and fruit flies, while diseases can range from fungal infections to bacterial issues. Regular monitoring is essential to catch any problems early. Integrated pest management (IPM) strategies can help control pests and diseases. This approach combines cultural practices, biological controls, and, if necessary, chemical treatments.

For example, using organic pest control methods, such as introducing beneficial insects or using insecticidal soap, can help manage pests without harming the environment. Proper spacing and pruning improve air circulation and reduce disease risk. If chemical treatments are needed, always follow label instructions and consider organic options to minimize environmental impact.

HARVESTING AND ENJOYING YOUR BERRIES

Harvesting berries at the right time is crucial for optimal flavor and quality. Most berries are ready to harvest when they have reached their full color and are slightly soft to the touch. For example, blueberries should be fully blue and easily come off the bush when gently pulled. Raspberries and blackberries should be harvested when they are fully colored and come off the plant easily. Grapes are ready to harvest when they have reached their full color and taste sweet.

Use a gentle hand when harvesting to avoid damaging the plants or the fruit. For most berries, you can simply pick them by hand, being careful not to crush or bruise the fruit. Freshly harvested berries can be enjoyed immediately or stored in the refrigerator for a few days. Many berries can also be frozen or preserved through canning, allowing you to enjoy them long after the growing season has ended.

LONG-TERM SUSTAINABILITY AND BENEFITS

Berry bushes and vines contribute to long-term sustainability in several ways. They provide a renewable source of fresh fruit, reducing the need for store-bought produce and minimizing packaging waste. Berry plants also support biodiversity by attracting pollinators like bees and butterflies, which benefit the entire garden ecosystem. Additionally, berry plants can help improve soil health by adding organic matter through leaf litter and root growth.

CHAPTER 11

HERBS AND MEDICINAL PLANTS

CULINARY HERBS: BASIL, MINT, ROSEMARY

Planting culinary herbs in a survival garden is not only practical but also adds a flavorful and aromatic dimension to your garden. Herbs like basil, mint, and rosemary are invaluable for enhancing your meals, offering medicinal benefits, and contributing to a self-sufficient lifestyle. Each of these herbs has unique growing requirements and uses, making them excellent choices for any survival garden. Here's how you can successfully incorporate these herbs into your garden.

BASIL: THE VERSATILE HERB

Basil is a popular culinary herb known for its aromatic leaves and distinctive flavor, which is a staple in many dishes, from pesto to salads. It's relatively easy to grow, making it an ideal choice for both novice and experienced gardeners.

Growing Conditions: Basil thrives in warm temperatures and full sun. It requires at least 6-8 hours of direct sunlight per day to grow well. The soil should be well-drained and rich in organic matter. Basil prefers a slightly acidic to neutral soil pH, ideally between 6.0 and 7.0.

Planting: Start basil seeds indoors 6-8 weeks before the last frost date if you're in a colder climate, or sow them directly in the garden once the danger of frost has passed and the soil has warmed up. Space the plants about 12 inches apart to allow for their full growth. Basil can also be grown in containers, which makes it a great option for those with limited garden space.

Care: Water basil regularly, keeping the soil consistently moist but not waterlogged. Avoid overhead watering to minimize the risk of fungal diseases. Pinch off the tips of the plants regularly to encourage bushier growth and prevent them from flowering too early. Once basil starts to flower, the leaves can become bitter. Harvest leaves as needed, and be sure to use them fresh for the best flavor.

MINT: THE HARDY HERB

Mint is a hardy perennial herb that spreads vigorously and is known for its refreshing flavor and medicinal properties. It's an excellent addition to any survival garden due to its ease of growth and versatility.

Growing Conditions: Mint prefers partial shade but can also tolerate full sun in cooler climates. It thrives in well-drained, moist soil with a pH between 6.0 and 7.0. Mint is quite adaptable and can grow in a variety of soil types, but it performs best in rich, loamy soil.

Planting: Mint is often grown from divisions or cuttings rather than seeds, as it can be difficult to start from seed. Plant mint in a container or garden bed with good drainage to control its aggressive spreading. If planting in the garden, consider using a barrier like a large pot or garden edging to keep mint from overtaking other plants. Space mint plants about 18-24 inches apart to allow for their spreading habit.

Care: Mint requires regular watering to keep the soil moist. It can be quite resilient and doesn't usually require much additional care. However, to maintain its best flavor and prevent disease, it's important to provide good air circulation around the plants. Mint can also be harvested throughout the growing season. Simply cut the stems as needed, and avoid removing more than one-third of the plant at a time to ensure continued growth.

ROSEMARY: THE AROMATIC EVERGREEN

Rosemary is a woody perennial herb known for its aromatic leaves and ability to withstand dry conditions. It adds a robust flavor to many dishes and has been used traditionally for its medicinal properties.

Growing Conditions: Rosemary requires full sun and well-drained soil with a pH between 6.0 and 7.0. It thrives in hot, dry conditions and is not tolerant of heavy or wet soils. In colder climates, rosemary is often grown as an annual or in containers that can be moved indoors during the winter.

Planting: Start rosemary from seeds indoors 8-10 weeks before the last frost or purchase young plants from a nursery. Rosemary can be grown in garden beds or containers, but make sure to provide good drainage. Space plants about 12-18 inches apart to allow for their mature size. If growing in containers, use a potting mix designed for Mediterranean herbs and ensure the container has good drainage.

Care: Rosemary is relatively low-maintenance but requires consistent watering, particularly during dry spells. Allow the soil to dry out between waterings, as rosemary is prone to root rot in overly moist conditions. Prune rosemary regularly to encourage a bushier growth habit and to prevent it from becoming leggy. Harvest the leaves as needed, and use them fresh for the best flavor.

INTEGRATING HERBS INTO YOUR GARDEN

Incorporating basil, mint, and rosemary into your survival garden not only enhances your culinary options but also supports your self-sufficiency goals. These herbs are not only useful for cooking but can also serve as natural pest repellents and ground cover in your garden. For instance, mint can deter pests like ants and rodents, while rosemary is known to repel mosquitoes.

Consider planting these herbs in dedicated beds or containers where they can thrive without competing with other plants. Companion planting is also beneficial; for example, basil can be planted near tomatoes to enhance their flavor and deter pests. Mint can provide ground cover around other plants to help retain soil moisture and suppress weeds, though it's best to manage its spread to prevent it from overtaking other areas.

For harvest times, all herbs are best harvested in the morning prior to the sun hitting the foliage. This is the time when the essential oils are the highest and the harvested yield will ensure you can benefit from the higher saturation.

MEDICINAL HERBS AND THEIR USES

Medicinal herbs are a cornerstone of survival gardening, offering both practical and health benefits. Integrating these herbs into your garden enhances your self-sufficiency because it reduces your reliance on store bought medications and also provides natural remedies for various ailments. Here's a look at some key medicinal herbs and their uses, along with tips for cultivating them in your survival garden.

ECHINACEA

Often referred to as coneflower, echinacea is renowned for its immune-boosting properties. It is commonly used to prevent or treat colds and flu, and it can also help with wound healing due to its anti-inflammatory and antimicrobial effects. Echinacea can be used in teas, tinctures, or as a topical application for minor cuts and scrapes.

Growing Echinacea: Echinacea prefers full sun to partial shade and well-drained soil with a pH between 6.0 and 7.0. It's a hardy perennial that can tolerate drought once established. Start seeds indoors 8-10 weeks before the last frost or sow them directly in the garden after the danger of frost has passed. Space plants about 12-18 inches apart to allow for their mature size. Echinacea is relatively low-maintenance, but it benefits from occasional watering during dry spells and can be divided every few years to maintain vigor.

LAVENDER

Lavender is not only valued for its soothing fragrance but also for its medicinal properties. It's often used to alleviate anxiety, insomnia, and digestive issues. Lavender can also be applied topically to soothe minor burns, insect bites, and skin irritations. Its essential oil is widely used in aromatherapy and as a calming agent.

Growing Lavender: Lavender thrives in full sun and well-drained soil with a pH between 6.5 and 7.5. It requires minimal watering once established, making it ideal for gardens with less frequent rainfall. Start lavender from seeds indoors or purchase young plants from a nursery. Space plants about 18-24 inches apart to ensure good air circulation. Lavender prefers a dry environment, so avoid overhead watering and use mulch to prevent soil erosion.

PEPPERMINT

Peppermint is a versatile herb used to aid digestion, relieve headaches, and soothe sore muscles. It has cooling and anti-inflammatory properties, making it useful for treating digestive discomfort, nausea, and respiratory issues. Peppermint tea is a common remedy for upset stomachs and indigestion.

Growing Peppermint: Peppermint prefers partial shade to full sun and well-drained, moist soil with a pH between 6.0 and 7.0. It can be invasive, so consider growing it in containers or using barriers to control its spread. Start peppermint from divisions or cuttings rather than seeds, as it propagates more easily this way. Space plants about 18-24 inches apart to manage its spreading habit. Regularly water peppermint to keep the soil moist, and harvest leaves as needed.

CHAMOMILE

Chamomile is well-known for its calming effects and is commonly used to treat anxiety, insomnia, and digestive issues. It also has anti-inflammatory and antimicrobial properties, making it useful for soothing skin irritations and minor wounds. Chamomile tea is a popular remedy for relaxation and improving sleep quality.

Growing Chamomile: Chamomile thrives in full sun and well-drained soil with a pH between 6.0 and 7.0. It's an annual herb that can be grown from seeds sown directly in the garden or started indoors. Space plants about 8-12 inches apart to allow for their mature size. Chamomile requires regular watering to keep the soil moist but not waterlogged. Harvest the flowers when they are fully open and dry them for later use.

CALENDULA

Calendula, also known as marigold, is valued for its anti-inflammatory and antimicrobial properties. It is commonly used to soothe skin irritations, minor wounds, and rashes. Calendula is also used in tinctures and salves for its healing properties and can be applied topically to promote skin health.

Growing Calendula: Calendula prefers full sun to partial shade and well-drained soil with a pH between 6.0 and 7.0. It's an annual herb that can be started from seeds sown directly in the garden or started indoors. Space plants about 6-12 inches apart to allow for their mature size. Calendula requires regular watering to keep the soil moist and benefits from deadheading to prolong blooming. Harvest flowers when they are fully open and dry them for later use.

THYME

Thyme is a hardy herb known for its antiseptic and antimicrobial properties. It is often used to treat respiratory issues, digestive problems, and as a natural remedy for coughs and colds. Thyme can also be used as a culinary herb to enhance flavor in a variety of dishes.

Growing Thyme: Thyme thrives in full sun and well-drained soil with a pH between 6.0 and 7.0. It's a hardy perennial that can tolerate drought once established. Start thyme from seeds indoors or purchase young plants from a nursery. Space plants about 12-18 inches apart to ensure good air circulation. Thyme requires minimal watering and benefits from occasional pruning to maintain its shape and vigor.

Integrating Medicinal Herbs into Your Garden

Incorporating medicinal herbs into your survival garden offers numerous benefits, from providing natural remedies to enhancing your overall self-sufficiency. When planning your garden, consider grouping herbs with similar growing requirements together to make care and maintenance easier. You can also use companion planting to benefit the garden ecosystem; for example, planting lavender near other herbs can help repel pests and attract beneficial insects.

HARVESTING AND USING MEDICINAL HERBS

Harvesting medicinal herbs at the right time is crucial for maximizing their therapeutic properties. Generally, herbs should be harvested in the morning after the dew has dried but before the heat of the day causes the essential oils to dissipate. For most herbs, the leaves and flowers are the primary parts used for medicinal purposes. Use clean, sharp scissors or pruning shears to harvest, and handle the plants gently to avoid damaging them.

After harvesting, herbs can be used fresh or dried for later use. Dry herbs by spreading them out in a well-ventilated area away from direct sunlight. Once dried, store them in airtight containers in a cool, dark place to preserve their potency. Many medicinal herbs can be used to make teas, tinctures, salves, and poultices, depending on their specific properties and your needs.

LONG-TERM SUSTAINABILITY AND BENEFITS

Growing medicinal herbs contributes to long-term sustainability by reducing reliance on store-bought medications and providing natural remedies for various health issues. These herbs also support biodiversity by attracting beneficial insects and contributing to a balanced garden ecosystem. Additionally, growing your own medicinal herbs can be a cost-effective way to access high-quality, natural remedies.

GROWING AND HARVESTING HERBS

Growing and harvesting herbs is a fulfilling aspect of gardening that offers numerous benefits. Selecting the right herbs is the first step in creating a successful herb garden. Consider your local climate, soil type, and the specific needs of each herb. For instance, some herbs thrive in full sun while others prefer partial shade. It's also important to select herbs based on your culinary and medicinal preferences. Popular choices include basil, mint, rosemary, thyme, chives, parsley, and cilantro, each offering unique flavors and benefits.

Planting herbs involves choosing the right site and preparing the soil. Most herbs prefer a sunny location with at least 6-8 hours of sunlight per day and well-drained soil. If your soil is heavy or clayey, using raised beds or containers can improve drainage and provide a better growing environment. Prepare the soil by incorporating organic matter such as compost to enhance fertility and structure. The ideal soil pH for most herbs ranges from 6.0 to 7.0. Herbs can be started from seeds, transplants, or divisions, depending on the species. Follow specific planting instructions for each herb, and ensure proper spacing to allow for mature growth.

Watering and fertilizing are crucial for healthy herb growth. Herbs generally require consistent moisture but are sensitive to overwatering, which can lead to root rot. Water herbs when the top inch of soil feels dry, and use a soaker hose or drip irrigation to provide gentle, steady moisture. Most herbs do not require heavy fertilization; a light application of balanced fertilizer or compost in the spring is usually sufficient. Over-fertilizing can result in excessive foliage growth at the expense of flavor and essential oils.

Maintaining herb plants involves regular pruning and monitoring for pests and diseases. Pruning helps to encourage bushier growth and prevents herbs from becoming leggy. Harvest herbs just before they begin to flower, as this is when their flavor and medicinal properties are most concentrated. Use sharp scissors or pruning shears to cut leaves or stems, and avoid removing more than one-third of the plant at a time to ensure continued growth. Keep an eye out for common pests like aphids and spider mites, and manage diseases by ensuring good air circulation and avoiding overhead watering.

Harvesting herbs at the right time and using the correct methods is essential for preserving their flavor and medicinal properties. The best time to harvest is in the morning after the dew has dried but before the heat of the day causes essential oils to dissipate. Pinch or cut stems just above a leaf node to encourage branching. For larger herbs, such as rosemary and lavender, cut back stems but leave enough foliage to support continued growth. After harvesting, herbs can be used fresh or preserved. To dry herbs, tie small bundles and hang them in a well-ventilated, dark area. Once dried, store them in airtight containers away from light. Freezing herbs by chopping them and placing them in ice cube trays with water or oil is another effective preservation method.

Using herbs involves incorporating them into your culinary and medicinal routines. Fresh herbs can enhance the flavor of dishes when added just before serving, while dried herbs are best used earlier in the cooking process. Experiment with different herbs to discover new flavor profiles and recipes. For medicinal purposes, herbs can be used to make teas, tinctures, and salves. Follow appropriate recipes and guidelines for each herb to ensure safe and effective use. Consulting with a healthcare provider before using herbs medicinally is advisable, especially if you have existing health conditions or are taking other medications.

Integrating herbs into your garden design can maximize their benefits. Plant herbs in dedicated beds or containers to keep them organized and accessible. Consider companion planting, which pairs herbs with vegetables or flowers that complement their growth. For example, basil can help deter pests that target tomatoes, and rosemary can attract beneficial insects.

PART 3
GARDEN MAINTENANCE AND PROBLEM-SOLVING

CHAPTER 12

PEST AND DISEASE MANAGEMENT

IDENTIFYING COMMON PESTS
AND DISEASES

When cultivating a survival garden, the goal is to grow a self-sustaining supply of food and medicinal plants, which means keeping the garden healthy and productive is crucial. Unfortunately, pests and diseases can pose significant challenges, potentially reducing yields or even wiping out crops. Understanding the common pests and diseases that might plague your garden, along with the less common ones, can help you implement preventive measures and respond effectively if issues arise.

1. APHIDS (COMMON)

Aphids are tiny, soft-bodied insects that can be green, black, brown, or pink. They cluster on the undersides of leaves and stems, feeding on plant sap, which weakens the plant and stunts growth. Aphids excrete a sticky substance called honeydew, which attracts ants and can lead to sooty mold growth. They're particularly fond of leafy greens, beans, and fruiting plants like tomatoes and peppers. To manage aphids, introduce beneficial insects like ladybugs, spray plants with a strong stream of water to dislodge them, or use insecticidal soap.

2. CABBAGE WORMS (COMMON)

Cabbage worms are the larvae of white butterflies, and they primarily target members of the brassica family, including cabbage, broccoli, and kale. These green caterpillars chew large holes in leaves and can quickly decimate a crop if not controlled. Handpicking, using floating row covers to prevent egg-laying, and introducing natural predators like parasitic wasps are effective control methods.

3. POWDERY MILDEW (COMMON)

Powdery mildew is a fungal disease that appears as a white or gray powdery coating on the leaves and stems of plants. It affects a wide range of plants, including cucumbers, squash, and herbs like basil. The fungus thrives in warm, dry conditions but requires humidity to germinate, making it a frequent issue in many gardens. To prevent and manage powdery mildew, ensure good air circulation by spacing plants properly, avoid overhead watering, and apply a fungicide if necessary.

4. TOMATO HORNWORMS (COMMON)

Tomato hornworms are large, green caterpillars with a horn-like projection on their rear end. They feed on the foliage, stems, and sometimes the fruits of tomato plants, and they can cause significant damage if not controlled. These pests are often hard to spot due to their excellent camouflage. Handpicking is the most effective control method, but introducing natural predators like parasitic wasps can also help keep their populations in check.

5. SLUGS AND SNAILS (COMMON)

Slugs and snails are notorious for munching on the tender leaves of young plants, especially during wet or humid conditions. They leave behind ragged holes in leaves and a telltale slimy trail. They particularly love leafy greens and strawberries. To manage slugs and snails, use barriers like copper tape, set out beer traps to lure and drown them, or handpick them in the evening or early morning when they're most active.

6. SPIDER MITES (COMMON)

Spider mites are tiny, spider-like pests that feed on the undersides of leaves, causing stippling and yellowing. They thrive in hot, dry conditions and can infest a wide variety of plants, including beans, tomatoes, and strawberries. To manage spider mites, increase humidity around the plants by misting them, use insecticidal soap, or introduce predatory mites that feed on spider mites.

7. BLIGHT (COMMON)

Blight is a term used to describe various plant diseases caused by fungi or bacteria, leading to the rapid yellowing, browning, and death of leaves, stems, and fruits. Late blight, which affects tomatoes and potatoes, is particularly devastating and can destroy an entire crop within days under the right conditions. Preventive measures include using disease-resistant varieties, rotating crops, and applying fungicides when necessary.

8. SQUASH BUGS (MODERATELY COMMON)

Squash bugs are shield-shaped insects that primarily target squash, pumpkins, and cucumbers. They feed by sucking sap from the leaves, causing wilting and eventually leading to plant death if the infestation is severe. Squash bugs also transmit diseases like cucurbit yellow vine disease. Control measures include handpicking, using row covers, and planting resistant varieties.

9. FUSARIUM WILT (MODERATELY COMMON)

Fusarium wilt is a soil-borne fungal disease that affects a wide range of plants, including tomatoes, peppers, and cucumbers. It causes the yellowing and wilting of leaves, often starting on one side of the plant. The fungus blocks the plant's water-conducting tissues, leading to wilting and eventual death. Crop rotation and planting resistant varieties are key to managing fusarium wilt, as the fungus can persist in the soil for several years.

10. COLORADO POTATO BEETLES
(MODERATELY COMMON)

The Colorado potato beetle is a notorious pest of potatoes, but it also attacks other members of the nightshade family, such as tomatoes and eggplants. The adult beetles and their larvae feed on the foliage, which can significantly reduce yields. Handpicking beetles and larvae, applying insecticidal soap, and rotating crops can help control their populations.

11. DOWNY MILDEW *(LESS COMMON)*

Downy mildew is a fungal disease that appears as yellowish spots on the upper leaf surface and a grayish, downy growth on the underside. It affects a variety of plants, including cucumbers, lettuce, and brassicas. Unlike powdery mildew, downy mildew thrives in cool, moist conditions. To manage it, ensure good air circulation, avoid overhead watering, and apply appropriate fungicides.

12. CUTWORMS *(LESS COMMON)*

Cutworms are the larvae of various moth species and are most damaging at night. They cut down young seedlings at the soil level, which can be devastating to newly planted gardens. These pests are particularly troublesome for crops like beans, lettuce, and tomatoes. Preventive measures include using collars around seedlings, handpicking, and applying diatomaceous earth around the base of plants.

13. VERTICILLIUM WILT (LESS COMMON)

Verticillium wilt is another soil-borne fungal disease that affects a wide range of plants, including tomatoes, eggplants, and potatoes. It causes wilting, yellowing, and stunted growth, often affecting one side of the plant. Like fusarium wilt, verticillium can persist in the soil, so crop rotation and planting resistant varieties are essential for management.

14. FLEA BEETLES (LESS COMMON)

Flea beetles are tiny, jumping beetles that chew small holes in leaves, creating a shot-hole appearance. They target a variety of crops, including radishes, eggplants, and leafy greens. While their damage is usually minor, heavy infestations can stunt young plants. Using row covers, planting trap crops, and applying neem oil can help manage flea beetle populations.

15. ROOT-KNOT NEMATODES
(LEAST COMMON)

Root-knot nematodes are microscopic worms that infect the roots of plants, causing the formation of galls or knots that interfere with water and nutrient uptake. Affected plants often appear stunted and may wilt despite adequate watering. These pests are difficult to control once established, so preventive measures, such as crop rotation, solarization, and planting resistant varieties, are crucial.

16. CLUBROOT
(LEAST COMMON)

Clubroot is a soil-borne disease that primarily affects members of the brassica family, including cabbage, broccoli, and kale. It causes swelling and distortion of the roots, leading to stunted growth and yellowing of leaves. Clubroot thrives in acidic soils, so maintaining a neutral pH through lime application can help prevent it. Crop rotation and using resistant varieties are also effective management strategies.

17. LEAFMINERS
(LEAST COMMON)

Leafminers are the larvae of various insects that burrow between the upper and lower surfaces of leaves, creating winding trails or blotches. While their damage is mostly cosmetic, heavy infestations can weaken plants and reduce yields. Leafminers target a wide range of crops, including spinach, beets, and tomatoes. Remove and destroy affected leaves, use row covers, and apply insecticidal soap or neem oil to manage infestations.

18. BLACK ROT
(LEAST COMMON)

Black rot is a bacterial disease that primarily affects brassicas, such as cabbage and broccoli. It causes yellow V-shaped lesions on the edges of leaves, which eventually turn black and spread inward. The bacteria are spread by water, so avoid overhead watering and handle plants carefully to prevent wounding. Crop rotation and using disease-free seeds are key preventive measures.

ORGANIC PEST CONTROL METHODS

When it comes to managing pests in your garden, turning to natural and organic methods can be highly effective while also being environmentally friendly. These approaches not only keep your plants healthy and thriving but also ensure that the ecosystem in and around your garden remains balanced. Organic pest control emphasizes prevention, biodiversity, and the use of natural materials to create a garden environment where pests are less likely to cause significant harm. Here are some natural and organic ways to keep those pesky invaders at bay:

1 → Companion Planting

One of the most popular natural methods to control pests is companion planting. This involves planting certain crops together that mutually benefit each other. For example, marigolds are often planted alongside tomatoes because they can repel nematodes, aphids, and even tomato hornworms. Similarly, planting basil near your tomatoes can improve their flavor and deter pests like flies and mosquitoes.

2 → Attracting Beneficial Insects

Not all insects are bad for your garden—some are actually your allies. Ladybugs, for instance, feast on aphids, while lacewings and hoverflies target a variety of other harmful insects. You can draw these helpful critters to your garden by planting flowers like dill, fennel, and yarrow, which provide them with nectar and pollen. Additionally, creating a diverse garden environment with plenty of flowering plants encourages these insects to take up residence, providing long-term pest control.

3 ⟶ Neem Oil

Neem oil is a potent natural insecticide derived from the seeds of the neem tree. It works by interfering with the life cycle of pests, including aphids, whiteflies, and spider mites, making it difficult for them to feed, grow, and reproduce. Neem oil is also effective against certain fungal diseases like powdery mildew. To use neem oil, mix it with water and a small amount of dish soap, then spray it onto the affected plants. This treatment should be applied during cooler parts of the day, such as early morning or late evening, to prevent leaf burn and to protect beneficial insects that are more active during the day.

4 ⟶ Diatomaceous Earth

Diatomaceous earth is a natural powder made from the fossilized remains of tiny, aquatic organisms called diatoms. It is an effective organic pest control solution because it kills insects by dehydrating them. When pests like ants, slugs, or beetles come into contact with diatomaceous earth, it damages their exoskeletons, leading to their death. To use, simply dust the powder around the base of your plants or on the soil where you've noticed pest activity. However, it's important to reapply it after rain or watering, as moisture reduces its effectiveness.

5 ⟶ Organic Sprays

Insecticidal soaps and horticultural oils are commonly used organic sprays that can help control pests in your garden. Insecticidal soap, made from natural fatty acids, works by breaking down the outer layer of soft-bodied insects like aphids and spider mites, leading to their dehydration. Horticultural oils, such as those made from neem or other plant-based oils, smother pests and can be effective against insects at all life stages, from eggs to adults. These sprays are best applied in the morning or evening to minimize the risk of harming beneficial insects and to avoid plant damage from the sun.

6 ⟶ Row Covers

Row covers are lightweight fabrics that can be draped over plants to protect them from pests while allowing sunlight, water, and air to pass through. These covers create a physical barrier that keeps pests, such as cabbage worms, flea beetles, and squash bugs, away from your plants. Row covers are particularly useful for protecting young seedlings, which are more vulnerable to pest attacks. Additionally, they can help reduce the spread of diseases by preventing infected insects from reaching healthy plants.

7 ⟶ Beneficial Nematodes

Beneficial nematodes are microscopic worms that live in the soil and attack the larvae of many soil-dwelling pests, such as grubs, root weevils, and cutworms. These nematodes enter the pest larvae, release bacteria that kill the host, and then reproduce inside the dead pest. Applying beneficial nematodes to your garden soil can provide long-lasting control of these hard-to-manage pests. Because they are living organisms, it's important to apply them when the soil is moist and to keep the soil watered to ensure their survival.

8 → Handpicking

For smaller gardens, handpicking pests off your plants can be surprisingly effective. This method is particularly useful for dealing with larger, more visible pests like caterpillars, beetles, and slugs. Simply inspect your plants regularly, and when you find pests, pick them off and dispose of them. While this method can be time-consuming, it's an immediate and chemical-free way to reduce pest populations.

9 → Natural Predators and Wildlife

Encouraging birds, frogs, toads, and other wildlife to visit your garden can also help control pests naturally. Birds, for example, feed on insects, caterpillars, and grubs. These natural predators are easily attracted by a bird friendly environment with bird feeders, birdbaths and nesting boxes. Frogs and toads, which feed on a variety of insects and slugs, can be encouraged by adding a small water feature or a shaded, moist area in your garden. Snakes and lizards, often feared by gardeners, are also beneficial as they help control rodents and larger insect pests.

10 → Baking Soda and Vinegar

Baking soda and vinegar are common household items that can be used to create natural pest repellents. A simple mixture of baking soda and water can be used as a spray to prevent fungal diseases like powdery mildew on plants. Vinegar, on the other hand, can be used as an insect repellent or a weed killer. A mixture of vinegar and water sprayed on the leaves of plants can deter pests like ants, aphids, and spiders. However, vinegar is acidic, so it should be used sparingly and with caution to avoid damaging your plants.

11 → Garlic and Hot Pepper Sprays

Garlic and hot pepper sprays are effective natural insect repellents. These sprays can deter a wide range of pests, including aphids, beetles, and caterpillars. To make a garlic spray, crush a few garlic cloves and steep them in water overnight. Strain the mixture and add a few drops of dish soap before spraying it on your plants. Hot pepper spray can be made by blending hot peppers with water and a bit of soap. These sprays work by irritating the pests, causing them to avoid the treated plants.

12 → Trap Crops

Trap crops are plants that are grown specifically to attract pests away from your main crops. For example, planting nasturtiums near your vegetable garden can attract aphids, keeping them away from your more valuable crops like tomatoes and peppers. Once the pests are concentrated on the trap crops, you can remove and destroy these plants, effectively reducing the pest population in your garden. Trap cropping can be a very effective strategy when combined with other organic pest control methods.

13 → Mulching

Mulching is another effective way to control pests and improve plant health. Organic mulches like straw, wood chips, or compost create a barrier that can help prevent soil-borne diseases from splashing onto your plants during rain or watering. Mulch also helps retain soil moisture, suppress weeds, and regulate soil temperature, all of which contribute to a healthier garden environment that is less conducive to pests. Additionally, certain types of mulch, such as cedar or cypress, can naturally repel insects.

14 → Crop Rotation

Crop rotation is a practice that involves changing the type of crops grown in a particular area each season. This helps disrupt the life cycles of pests that are specific to certain plants and reduces the buildup of soil-borne diseases. For example, if you grow tomatoes in one area of your garden this year, consider planting beans or lettuce in that area next year.

15 → Solarization

Solarization is a natural method of pest control that uses the sun's heat to kill soil-borne pests, diseases, and weed seeds. To solarize your soil, cover the area with a clear plastic sheet and leave it in place for 4-6 weeks during the hottest part of the summer. The heat trapped under the plastic raises the soil temperature to levels that are lethal to many pathogens and pests. Solarization is particularly effective in regions with hot summers and can be a great way to prepare your garden bed before planting.

DISEASE PREVENTION AND TREATMENT

Just like with pest control, adopting natural and organic methods can be highly effective while also being environmentally friendly. Disease prevention starts with good gardening practices, but even with the best care, some plants may still fall prey to disease. The key is to stay vigilant, recognize the signs early, and take appropriate action. Here's how you can prevent and treat diseases in your garden:

1 → 1. Start with Healthy Soil

Healthy soil is the foundation of a healthy garden. When your soil is rich in organic matter and well-draining, it provides an environment where plants can thrive and resist diseases. Composting is a great way to improve soil health by adding essential nutrients and beneficial microorganisms. Regularly test your soil to check for nutrient deficiencies or imbalances, and amend it as needed. Healthy soil encourages strong root systems, which are less likely to succumb to diseases.

2 → 2. Choose Disease-Resistant Varieties

When planning your garden, consider choosing plant varieties that are bred to resist common diseases. Many seed companies label these varieties with terms like "disease-resistant" or abbreviations that denote resistance to specific diseases, such as "VFN" (resistant to Verticillium wilt, Fusarium wilt, and nematodes). Planting disease-resistant varieties can significantly reduce the likelihood of disease outbreaks in your garden.

3 → 3. Practice Crop Rotation

Crop rotation is an effective strategy for preventing soil-borne diseases. Life cycles of pathogens can be disrupted during annual crop rotations. For example, if you grow tomatoes in one area of your garden this year, avoid planting tomatoes or other members of the nightshade family in that same spot next year. Instead, plant a different crop, such as beans or lettuce, to reduce the risk of disease.

4 → 4. Proper Plant Spacing and Air Circulation

Crowded plants are more susceptible to disease because they create a humid environment where pathogens can thrive. Proper spacing allows for good air circulation around plants, which helps prevent the spread of fungal diseases like powdery mildew and blight. When planting your garden, follow the recommended spacing guidelines for each plant variety. Additionally, consider pruning overcrowded foliage to further improve air circulation.

5 → 5. Watering Techniques

How and when you water your plants can significantly impact their susceptibility to disease. Watering early in the morning allows plants to dry off during the day, reducing the risk of fungal infections. Avoid overhead watering, as this can splash soil-borne pathogens onto leaves and create a moist environment that promotes disease. Instead, use drip irrigation or soaker hoses to deliver water directly to the soil, keeping the foliage dry.

6. Mulching

Mulching is a simple yet effective way to prevent diseases in your garden. Organic mulch, such as straw, wood chips, or compost, creates a barrier that prevents soil-borne pathogens from splashing onto the lower leaves of your plants during rain or watering. Mulch also helps retain soil moisture, regulate temperature, and suppress weeds, all of which contribute to a healthier garden environment. However, avoid piling mulch directly against the stems of plants, as this can create a damp environment that encourages rot.

7. Sanitation and Cleanliness

Maintaining a clean garden is essential for disease prevention. Remove and dispose of any diseased plants, fallen leaves, or debris promptly, as these can harbor pathogens that may spread to healthy plants. At the end of the growing season, clear out your garden beds and compost any healthy plant material. Clean and disinfect your gardening tools regularly to prevent the spread of diseases from one plant to another.

8. Monitor and Inspect Regularly

Regular monitoring is key to early detection and treatment of diseases. Inspect your plants frequently for signs of disease, such as yellowing leaves, spots, wilting, or unusual growth patterns. Early detection allows you to take swift action before the disease spreads throughout your garden. Keep a close eye on plants that are particularly susceptible to disease and act immediately if you notice any symptoms.

9. Natural Disease Treatments

If you do encounter a disease in your garden, there are several natural treatments you can use to manage it. Here are a few:

- Baking Soda Solution: Baking soda is a natural fungicide that can help control fungal diseases like powdery mildew and black spot. Mix 1 tablespoon of baking soda with 1 gallon of water and a few drops of liquid soap. Spray the solution on affected plants, making sure to cover both the tops and undersides of the leaves. Repeat every 7-10 days or after rain.

- Neem Oil: Neem oil is an organic treatment that works against a variety of fungal diseases, including rust, powdery mildew, and downy mildew. It also has insecticidal properties, making it a versatile addition to your garden toolkit. To use neem oil, mix it with water according to the package instructions and spray it on affected plants. Apply neem oil in the early morning or late evening to avoid harming beneficial insects.

- **Milk Spray:** Milk has been shown to be effective in treating powdery mildew. Mix 1 part milk (preferably skim or 2%) with 9 parts water and spray it on the affected plants. The proteins in milk help inhibit the growth of the fungus. Apply the milk spray once a week or after rain.

- **Copper-Based Sprays:** Copper-based fungicides are an organic option for treating a wide range of fungal and bacterial diseases. These sprays work by creating a protective barrier on the plant's surface, preventing the pathogen from spreading. However, use copper sprays sparingly, as excessive use can lead to copper buildup in the soil, which can be harmful to plants.

10. Encourage Beneficial Microorganisms

A healthy garden ecosystem includes beneficial microorganisms that help suppress disease-causing pathogens. These microorganisms can be encouraged by adding compost, compost tea, or other organic amendments to your soil. Mycorrhizal fungi, for example, form symbiotic relationships with plant roots, helping plants absorb nutrients while also protecting them from certain soil-borne diseases. Introducing beneficial bacteria and fungi into your garden can create a more resilient environment where diseases are less likely to take hold.

11. Solarization

Soil solarization is a technique that uses the sun's heat to kill soil-borne pathogens, weed seeds, and insects. This method is particularly useful for treating soil that has been affected by persistent diseases. To solarize your soil, cover the area with a clear plastic sheet and leave it in place for 4-6 weeks during the hottest part of the summer. The heat trapped under the plastic raises the soil temperature to levels that are lethal to many pathogens. After solarization, your soil will be healthier and better prepared for planting.

12. Use of Disease-Free Seeds and Transplants

Starting with disease-free seeds and transplants is an important step in preventing the introduction of diseases into your garden. Purchase seeds and plants from reputable sources that certify their products as disease-free. If you're starting seeds indoors, use sterile soil and containers to prevent contamination. When transplanting, inspect the plants for any signs of disease before placing them in your garden.

13. Avoid Over-Fertilization

While it's important to provide your plants with the nutrients they need, over-fertilization can actually make them more susceptible to disease. Excess nitrogen, in particular, can promote lush, tender growth that is more attractive to pests and more prone to fungal infections. Follow the recommended fertilization guidelines for your plants, and use organic fertilizers that release nutrients slowly and steadily.

14 →

14. Rotate Fungicides

If you use organic fungicides to treat plant diseases, it's important to rotate the types of fungicides you use to prevent the pathogens from developing resistance. Just as bacteria can become resistant to antibiotics, plant pathogens can become resistant to fungicides if the same product is used repeatedly.

15 →

15. Quarantine New Plants

Before introducing new plants to your garden, especially if they are purchased from a nursery or another garden, consider quarantining them for a few weeks in a separate area. This allows you to monitor the plants for any signs of disease or pests before they have the chance to spread to your existing plants. If any issues arise, you can treat the new plants without risking the health of your entire garden.

16 →

16. Proper Disposal of Infected Plant Material

When a plant becomes infected with a disease, it's important to remove and dispose of the affected plant material properly. Do not compost diseased plants, as the pathogens may survive the composting process and be reintroduced to your garden when you use the compost. Instead, dispose of the infected material in the trash or burn it, if permitted in your area.

CHAPTER 13

GARDEN CARE AND MAINTENANCE

MULCHING AND WEED CONTROL

Mulching and weed control are two of the most essential practices in maintaining a healthy and productive garden, especially in the context of a survival garden where every plant and every bit of soil fertility counts. While they might seem like simple tasks, the benefits they bring to your garden are profound, making them well worth the effort. Let's dive into the details of how mulching and weed control work together to create a thriving garden ecosystem.

UNDERSTANDING MULCHING: WHAT IT IS AND WHY IT MATTERS

Mulching is the process of covering the soil around your plants with a protective layer of material, known as mulch. This can be organic materials like straw, leaves, grass clippings, compost, or wood chips. Inorganic materials such as black plastic or landscape fabric can also be used but they come with their set of caveats. Black plastic is often used for its ability to warm the soil early in the growing season, which can promote faster plant growth, but it doesn't allow water or air to penetrate, resulting in suffocation for the roots because an exchange of gases cannot occur with the surrounding microbes, so irrigation and aeration needs to be adjusted accordingly; landscape fabric, on the other hand, allows water and air to reach the soil while still suppressing weed growth, making it a good option for long-term garden use. Your choice should wholly depend on your long- and short-term goals for the garden.

The primary purpose of mulch is to protect and enhance the soil, but its benefits extend far beyond that.

One of the most significant benefits of mulching is its ability to retain moisture in the soil. This is particularly important in a survival garden, where water conservation might be crucial. Less frequent watering not only saves water but also reduces the stress on plants, promoting healthier growth.

Mulch acts as an insulating layer, helping to regulate soil temperature. In the summer, it keeps the soil cooler by blocking direct sunlight, which can prevent the roots from overheating. In the winter, mulch helps retain soil warmth, protecting plants from frost damage. This temperature regulation creates a more stable environment for plant roots, reducing stress and encouraging consistent growth throughout the growing season.

As organic mulch materials break down, they decompose and gradually add organic matter to the soil. This process improves soil structure, enhances its ability to hold water, and provides essential nutrients to the plants. Over time, the soil becomes more fertile and better able to support healthy plant growth. Inorganic mulches don't break down in the same way but can still protect the soil surface and reduce erosion.

Mulching is one of the most effective natural methods of weed control. Even if weeds do manage to sprout, the mulch layer makes it harder for them to establish a strong foothold, allowing you to easily pull them out before they become a problem. This is particularly useful in a survival garden, where you want to minimize competition for resources like water and nutrients.

Heavy rains and wind can lead to soil erosion, washing away valuable top-soil and nutrients. Mulch helps to anchor the soil in place, reducing the impact of erosion. This is especially important on sloped areas of your garden, where erosion can be more pronounced.

TYPES OF MULCH AND THEIR SPECIFIC BENEFITS

Choosing the right type of mulch for your garden depends on your specific needs, the climate, and the crops you're growing. Here's a breakdown of different types of mulch and their unique advantages:

Organic Mulch

- **Straw:** Excellent for vegetable gardens, straw is lightweight and easy to spread. It decomposes relatively quickly, adding organic matter to the soil. It's particularly good for keeping fruits and vegetables clean and dry, as it provides a barrier between the soil and the plants.

- **Leaves:** Shredded leaves are a readily available and cost-effective mulch. They break down slowly, providing long-term soil improvement. Leaf mulch is particularly beneficial in woodland or forest garden settings, where it mimics the natural leaf litter found on the forest floor.

- **Grass Clippings:** Fresh grass clippings are high in nitrogen, making them a good choice for mulching around heavy feeders like corn or squash. However, they can mat down and become slimy, so it's best to apply them in thin layers and allow them to dry out slightly before using.

- **Wood Chips:** Wood chips are a long-lasting mulch that breaks down slowly, adding organic matter to the soil over time. They are particularly useful around trees, shrubs, and perennial beds. However, avoid using fresh wood chips directly around vegetable plants, as they can tie up nitrogen in the soil as they decompose.

Inorganic Mulch

- **Black Plastic:** Black plastic mulch is effective for warming the soil in early spring and preventing weed growth. Accompanied by an underlying irrigation system, it's commonly used in vegetable gardens for crops like tomatoes and peppers. However, it doesn't add any nutrients to the soil and needs to be removed and disposed of at the end of the season.

- **Landscape Fabric:** This is a more permanent solution for weed control in areas like pathways or around perennial plants. Landscape fabric allows water and air to pass through while blocking sunlight from reaching weed seeds. It's often used in combination with a layer of organic mulch on top.

WEED CONTROL:
STRATEGIES FOR KEEPING YOUR GARDEN WEED-FREE

Weeds are the bane of every gardener's existence. They compete with your plants for nutrients, water, and light, and can quickly overtake a garden if left unchecked. Effective weed control is about more than just pulling weeds out when you see them; it involves a proactive approach that keeps weeds from becoming a problem in the first place.

As mentioned earlier, mulching is a powerful tool for weed suppression. Covering the soil during mulching prevents sunlight from reaching weed seeds, thereby reducing the number of weeds that germinate. For maximum effectiveness, apply a thick layer of mulch—at least 2 to 4 inches deep. Organic mulches, like straw or wood chips, are particularly good at suppressing weeds while also improving the soil over time.

Even with mulch, some weeds will inevitably find their way into your garden. Regular hand weeding is essential, especially in the early stages of weed growth when they are easiest to remove. The best time to weed is after a rain, when the soil is moist and the weeds pull out easily. Make sure to remove the entire root, especially for perennial weeds like dandelions, which can regrow from any root fragments left in the soil.

Hoeing is a traditional method of weed control that is particularly effective for annual weeds. Using a sharp hoe, you can cut weeds off at the soil surface, preventing them from growing back. Hoeing is best done on a dry day, as the severed weeds will dry out and die quickly, without rerooting in the soil. It's a fast and efficient way to keep weeds under control, especially in larger garden areas.

For particularly stubborn weeds, or to prepare a new garden bed, smothering can be an effective strategy. This involves covering the soil with a thick, opaque material like cardboard, newspaper, or a tarp, which blocks all light and effectively kills any weeds underneath. After a few weeks or months, the weeds will be dead, and you can remove the covering and plant in the now weed-free soil.

Weed control is also influenced by your planting strategy. Crop rotation can disrupt the life cycles of certain weeds by changing the type of plants grown in a particular area each year. Cover crops, such as clover or rye, can be grown in the off-season to outcompete weeds and improve soil health. When tilled under in the spring, they add organic matter to the soil while also suppressing weed growth.

One of the keys to effective weed control is preventing weeds from spreading in the first place. Always clean your tools after working in areas with weeds to avoid transferring seeds to other parts of your garden. Be cautious when introducing new soil, compost, or mulch, as these can sometimes contain weed seeds. If you're bringing in organic mulch, make sure it's well-aged or composted to minimize the risk of introducing weeds.

PRUNING AND TRAINING PLANTS

Pruning and training plants are two of the most vital practices in gardening, especially in a survival garden where maximizing the health, yield, and longevity of your crops is crucial. While these techniques might seem daunting at first, understanding the principles behind them can make a significant difference in the productivity of your garden.

UNDERSTANDING PRUNING: WHY IT'S IMPORTANT

Pruning is the selective removal of certain parts of a plant, such as branches, buds, or roots. The main goals of pruning are to improve plant health, control growth, enhance fruit or flower production, and maintain the plant's shape. In a survival garden, where every plant is grown with the intention of providing food or other essential resources, pruning becomes an essential practice to ensure that each plant is as productive and healthy as possible.

Pruning helps remove dead, diseased, or damaged parts of the plant, which can prevent the spread of diseases and pests. This improves the overall health of the plant and also reduces the likelihood of diseases spreading to other plants in your garden.

One of the key benefits of pruning is that it opens up the plant canopy, allowing better air circulation and sunlight penetration. Good air circulation reduces the risk of fungal diseases, which thrive in damp, stagnant conditions. Increased sunlight exposure ensures that all parts of the plant, including the lower branches, receive adequate light for photosynthesis, leading to more robust growth and higher yields.

For fruiting plants, pruning is essential to stimulate the production of fruiting wood and to manage the size and quality of the fruit. This is particularly important in fruit trees and berry bushes, where overgrowth can lead to smaller, less flavorful fruit.

Pruning helps control the size and shape of your plants, making them more manageable and ensuring they don't outgrow their space.

TRAINING PLANTS: SHAPING FOR SUCCESS

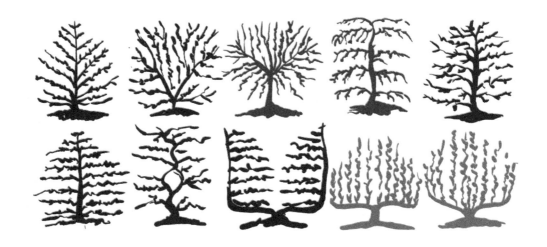

Training is the practice of guiding the growth of plants in specific directions or shapes. This is often done in conjunction with pruning and is particularly useful for vining plants, fruit trees, and shrubs. Training helps optimize space, increase yields, and make harvesting easier.

In a survival garden, efficient use of space is critical. Training plants to grow vertically, for example, allows you to make the most of limited ground space. Techniques like trellising, espalier (training trees against a wall or fence), and staking encourage plants to grow upwards rather than outwards, freeing up space for other crops. Vertical gardening is particularly useful for vining plants like tomatoes, cucumbers, and beans, which can be trained to climb supports.

For instance, training grapevines or espaliered fruit trees allows each branch to receive ample sunlight, promoting the growth of more fruit-bearing wood. Additionally, training can help evenly distribute the plant's energy, resulting in more uniform and higher-quality fruits or vegetables.

Training plants to grow in specific patterns or shapes can make them easier to harvest and maintain. For example, training tomato plants to grow on a trellis keeps the fruit off the ground, reducing the risk of rot and making it easier to see and pick ripe tomatoes. Similarly, training fruit trees into an espalier shape keeps the branches within easy reach, simplifying pruning, spraying, and harvesting.

PRACTICAL TIPS FOR PRUNING AND TRAINING

Getting started with pruning and training requires a bit of knowledge and practice, but the rewards are well worth the effort. Here are some practical insights to effectively prune and train your plant:

- The best time to prune most plants is during their dormant season, typically in late winter or early spring before new growth begins. Pruning during dormancy reduces the risk of shock and allows the plant to heal quickly when it starts growing again. However, some plants, like spring-flowering shrubs, should be pruned immediately after they bloom to avoid cutting off next year's flower buds.

- Having the right tools makes pruning much easier and more effective. A pair of sharp, clean pruning shears is essential for most tasks. For thicker branches, you may need loppers or a pruning saw. Always disinfect your tools before and after pruning to prevent the spread of disease. Sharp tools make cleaner cuts, which heal faster and reduce the risk of infection.

- When pruning, start by removing any dead, diseased, or damaged branches. This clears the way for healthier growth and reduces the risk of disease spreading to other parts of the plant. After removing these, you can focus on shaping the plant and thinning out crowded areas to improve air circulation and light penetration.

- The earlier you start training plants, the easier it is to guide their growth. Young, flexible branches are easier to bend and shape without breaking. Begin training young plants as soon as they are established, using supports like stakes, trellises, or wires to guide their growth. Regularly check and adjust the training to ensure the plant continues to grow in the desired direction.

- Pruning and training are ongoing tasks, not one-time jobs. Regular maintenance is key to keeping plants healthy and productive. Check your plants periodically and make small adjustments as needed, rather than waiting until problems arise. Consistent care helps prevent overgrowth and ensures that your plants remain well-shaped and manageable.

SEASONAL GARDEN TASKS

Managing a survival garden involves a careful rhythm of seasonal tasks that ensure your plants remain healthy and productive throughout the year. Each season brings its unique challenges and opportunities, and keeping up with these tasks can make the difference between a thriving garden and a struggling one.

SPRING

In spring, the garden begins to wake up from winter dormancy. It's essential to start by preparing the soil, which involves testing for pH levels and nutrient content. This allows you to amend the soil with compost or well-rotted manure, ensuring it is fertile and well-structured. Cleaning up any remaining plant debris from the previous season helps prevent diseases and pests. As the soil becomes workable, it's time to start seeds indoors for plants that need a head start, such as tomatoes and peppers, and to sow cool-season crops directly into the garden. Additionally, spring is a good time to prune dormant fruit trees and check garden structures for any necessary repairs.

SUMMER

As summer arrives, the focus shifts to maintaining the growth and health of your garden. The increased temperatures mean plants require more frequent watering. Efficient irrigation becomes crucial, and mulching helps retain moisture and reduce watering needs. Summer is also the peak time for weed and pest control; regularly check for weeds and remove them promptly to prevent competition for resources. Keep an eye out for pests and diseases, taking natural or organic measures to address any issues. Supporting plants that grow tall or produce heavy fruit with stakes or trellises is important to prevent damage. During this busy season, keep up with fertilizing to ensure plants receive the nutrients they need and start harvesting early crops as they ripen to encourage continued production.

FALL

Fall brings the harvest season and a time to prepare the garden for winter. Continue harvesting late-season crops, such as root vegetables and squash, and store them properly to ensure a supply of food through the colder months. Clean up garden beds by removing dead plant material and debris, which helps reduce the risk of pests and diseases overwintering in the soil. Adding compost or well-rotted manure to garden beds improves soil fertility for the next growing season. Planting cover crops like clover or rye in the fall enriches the soil and prevents erosion. If you have winter-hardy crops or bulbs, now is the time to plant them. Protect tender plants with row covers or cold frames to shield them from frost and harsh weather.

WINTER

Winter is a quieter time in the garden but offers a valuable opportunity for rest, reflection, and planning. Use this time to review the past season's successes and challenges, making notes for future improvements. Research new plants, techniques, or tools, and plan your garden layout and crop rotations for the upcoming year. Order seeds and supplies in advance to ensure you're ready for spring planting. Winter is also ideal for maintaining garden tools—cleaning and sharpening them so they're ready for use. Consider indoor gardening projects or building and repairing garden structures, like raised beds and trellises. Keeping a garden journal can be incredibly helpful for tracking your observations and planning for the next season.

CHAPTER 14

MAXIMIZING YIELD IN SMALL SPACES

VERTICAL GARDENING TECHNIQUES

Vertical gardening techniques are innovative strategies that allow gardeners to maximize space by growing plants upwards instead of outwards, making them particularly useful in confined areas or urban environments. Each technique offers unique benefits, enhancing both the aesthetic appeal and functionality of garden spaces. Here's a detailed look at various vertical gardening methods and the advantages they provide.

Trellises

Trellises are one of the most popular vertical gardening techniques, designed to support climbing plants and vining crops. Made from materials like wood, metal, or plastic, trellises come in various shapes and sizes, catering to different plant needs. The primary benefit of using trellises is space efficiency; by allowing plants to grow vertically, you free up ground space for other uses. Additionally, trellises improve air circulation around the plants, reducing the risk of fungal diseases and pests. This technique is ideal for plants such as tomatoes, cucumbers, and beans, which naturally climb and benefit from vertical support. Trellises also make harvesting easier by elevating crops and keeping them off the ground.

Arbors and Pergolas

Arbors and pergolas are larger vertical structures that offer substantial support for climbing and sprawling plants. Arbors are typically used as entranceways or garden features, while pergolas are freestanding structures that can cover dining areas or walkways. The major benefit of arbors and pergolas is their ability to create shaded spaces and visual focal points in the garden. They are particularly effective for supporting heavy or sprawling plants like grapes, kiwis, or flowering vines such as wisteria and climbing roses. These structures not only enhance the garden's aesthetic but also provide a functional outdoor space that can be enjoyed during warm weather.

Vertical Planters

Vertical planters are specially designed containers that allow you to grow plants in a vertical arrangement. These come in various forms, including wall-mounted pockets, hanging pots, and tiered shelves. Wall-mounted pockets are great for herbs, lettuce, and small flowers, while hanging pots are ideal for trailing plants like strawberries or cascading flowers. Tiered shelves or stackable planters create multiple planting levels, maximizing space in compact areas such as balconies or small yards. The benefits of vertical planters include efficient space utilization and ease of access for planting and maintenance. They also help to create a lush, green look in limited spaces, adding to the garden's visual appeal.

Green Walls

Green walls, or living walls, are sophisticated vertical gardens installed on building exteriors, interior walls, or freestanding panels. These systems use modular planting panels, hydroponic setups, or custom-built structures to support a wide variety of plants. Green walls offer numerous benefits, including improved insulation, enhanced air quality, and a striking visual element that can transform urban environments. They can support a diverse range of plants, from succulents to herbs, and are particularly useful for creating green spaces in areas where traditional gardens are not feasible. Additionally, green walls can contribute to energy savings by insulating buildings and reducing heat loss.

Espalier

<u>Espalier</u> is a technique used to train fruit trees and shrubs to grow flat against a wall or trellis. This method is ideal for maximizing space and creating decorative patterns while making plants more accessible for maintenance and harvesting. The primary benefit of espalier is its ability to integrate fruit trees and shrubs into garden walls, fences, or trellises, saving ground space and creating visually appealing forms. Espaliered plants are often used in formal gardens and can be arranged in various shapes, adding both functionality and beauty to the garden. This technique also simplifies care and harvesting, as the plants are more accessible and neatly arranged.

Hanging Gardens

<u>Hanging gardens</u> involve suspending plants from overhead structures, such as hanging baskets, macramé plant hangers, or repurposed items like old teacups. This technique is particularly useful for growing herbs, flowers, or small vegetables in compact spaces. Hanging gardens offer benefits like saving ground space and creating a visually interesting, cascading effect. They are also versatile, as you can use a variety of containers and arrangements to fit different spaces and styles. Hanging gardens are well-suited for adding greenery to indoor spaces, patios, or balconies, providing a fresh and vibrant look.

Wall Mounts

Wall-mounted shelves are practical for growing plants vertically in indoor spaces or small gardens. These shelves can be installed on any wall and used to hold pots or containers, allowing you to grow herbs, succulents, or small flowering plants. The benefits of wall-mounted shelves include efficient space utilization and ease of access to plants. This technique is ideal for integrating plants into indoor environments, such as kitchens or living rooms, where traditional ground space is limited.

Vertical Hydroponics

Vertical hydroponic systems are advanced setups that use a soilless growing method to cultivate plants in a vertical arrangement. These systems involve nutrient-rich water solutions that feed plants through a series of tubes or channels. The primary benefits of vertical hydroponics include precise control over nutrients and water, which can lead to faster growth and higher yields. These systems are particularly useful in commercial vertical farming but can be adapted for home use as well. Vertical hydroponic systems are ideal for growing a variety of crops in a compact space, offering a high level of efficiency and productivity.

INTENSIVE PLANTING METHODS

Intensive planting methods are transformative techniques that radically enhance the efficiency and productivity of gardening by making the most of available space and resources. These methods are designed to optimize the use of garden areas, whether they're large or small, by employing strategies that maximize crop yields and improve overall garden health. Here's a detailed exploration of several key intensive planting methods, their implementation, and the numerous benefits they offer.

SQUARE FOOT GARDENING

Square Foot Gardening is a highly efficient method that divides the garden space into square-foot sections, with each section designated for specific crops. This method enables gardeners to plant a variety of vegetables and herbs in a compact area by adhering to precise spacing guidelines. For example, one square foot might accommodate several radish plants, a single tomato, or a bunch of lettuce. The primary advantage of square foot gardening is its ability to maximize space utilization, leading to higher productivity in smaller areas. Additionally, this method reduces weed growth and simplifies garden maintenance, as each square foot is neatly organized and easy to manage. The efficiency of space usage also means fewer pathways are needed, which can further reduce the chances of weed infestation and make the garden easier to tend.

COMPANION PLANTING

Companion Planting is another intensive method where different plant species are grown together to benefit each other in various ways. This technique capitalizes on the natural relationships between plants to enhance growth, deter pests, and improve nutrient uptake. For instance, planting marigolds alongside tomatoes can repel harmful insects, while beans can fix nitrogen in the soil, benefiting corn planted nearby. Companion planting not only optimizes space but also fosters a balanced ecosystem within the garden. The strategic placement of plants can lead to healthier crops and reduce the need for chemical pest control.

INTERPLANTING

Interplanting, or intercropping, involves growing different crops together in the same area at various times or in alternating rows. This method allows for better use of space and resources by optimizing plant growth. For example, fast-growing crops like radishes can be planted between slower-growing crops like carrots, utilizing space that would otherwise remain empty while waiting for the slower crops to mature. Interplanting can improve soil health by reducing erosion and increasing biodiversity. It also helps in managing pest and disease pressures by creating a diverse planting environment that can disrupt pest cycles.

VERTICAL GARDENING

Vertical Gardening techniques, such as using trellises, vertical planters, and green walls, allow gardeners to grow plants upwards rather than outwards. Trellises support climbing plants like tomatoes and cucumbers, improving air circulation and making harvesting easier. **Vertical planters**, which can include wall-mounted pockets and tiered shelves, are perfect for growing herbs and small vegetables in confined spaces. Green walls, or living walls, use modular systems to support a variety of plants, creating lush, vertical gardens on walls or panels. The benefits of vertical gardening are manifold: it maximizes space, improves air flow around plants, and creates visually appealing features in the garden. This method is especially valuable in urban settings where horizontal space is limited but vertical space is available.

RAISED BED GARDENING

Raised Bed Gardening involves constructing garden beds that are elevated above ground, often using materials like wood or stone. These beds are filled with high-quality soil and compost, providing an optimal growing environment for plants. Raised beds offer several benefits, including improved drainage, reduced soil compaction, and enhanced soil fertility. They also facilitate easier access for planting, weeding, and harvesting, making garden maintenance more manageable. The elevated design of raised beds allows for denser planting, which can lead to higher yields in a smaller area. Additionally, raised beds can be designed to fit specific space constraints or aesthetic preferences, providing both functionality and visual appeal.

SUCCESSION PLANTING

Succession Planting is a technique that involves planting crops in a sequence to ensure a continuous harvest throughout the growing season. For instance, after harvesting early-season crops like peas, you might immediately plant a new crop of beans or lettuce. Succession planting helps in making efficient use of garden space and provides a steady supply of fresh produce. This method also allows for better management of seasonal variations and crop rotations, contributing to a more productive and diverse garden.

INTENSIVE ROW PLANTING

Intensive Row Planting focuses on growing crops in closely spaced rows, often narrower than traditional planting methods. This approach allows for a higher density of plants per unit area, which can lead to increased yields. Intensive row planting is particularly effective for crops like lettuce, spinach, and radishes, where dense planting can optimize space and improve soil fertility. The key benefits include efficient use of space and resources, as well as the potential for higher overall productivity. However, it's essential to manage spacing carefully to ensure adequate air circulation and prevent disease spread.

MULTI-LAYERED PLANTING

Multi-Layered Planting, also known as tiered planting, involves growing different types of plants at varying heights to maximize vertical space. This method combines ground-cover plants, low-growing vegetables, and taller crops to create a layered effect. For example, you might plant herbs and lettuce as a ground cover, followed by medium-height vegetables like peppers, and then taller crops like tomatoes or corn. Multi-layered planting can increase yield by utilizing space more effectively and allowing different plants to thrive in their respective layers. This technique also helps in managing light exposure and can enhance pest and disease management by creating a more complex and resilient plant environment.

INTERCROPPING FOR HIGH YIELDS

Intercropping, an advanced agricultural technique, is all about growing different types of crops in close proximity within the same space. This method maximizes the use of available land by strategically planting complementary crops together, rather than using traditional monoculture, where only one type of crop is grown over a large area. The primary goal of intercropping is to increase overall productivity and yield by harnessing the benefits of plant diversity.

One of the key advantages of intercropping is its ability to utilize space more efficiently. For example, fast-growing plants like radishes or lettuce can be grown alongside slower-maturing crops like carrots or beets. The fast-growers will be harvested before the slower plants require more space, allowing you to get multiple harvests from the same area within a single growing season. This strategic arrangement ensures that no space goes unused, which can lead to a higher yield per square foot compared to traditional single-crop planting.

Intercropping also enhances resource use efficiency. Different crops often have varying requirements for light, water, and nutrients. For instance, deep-rooted plants like carrots or radishes can be grown alongside shallow-rooted plants like onions or garlic. The deep roots of tomatoes can access nutrients and water deeper in the soil, while the shallow roots of onions or garlic utilize the upper soil layers. This efficient use of resources helps to improve soil health and can lead to better growth and yields for all crops involved.

Another significant benefit of intercropping is its ability to improve soil health and fertility. Certain crops, such as legumes, have the ability to fix atmospheric nitrogen into the soil, making it more fertile for subsequent crops. Planting legumes like beans or peas alongside other crops can enhance soil nitrogen levels, reducing the need for synthetic fertilizers. This natural fertilization improves soil structure and increases nutrient availability, leading to healthier plants and higher yields. Additionally, diverse plantings can help to reduce soil erosion and improve organic matter content in the soil, further enhancing soil health.

Pest and disease management is also more effective with intercropping. Growing a variety of plants together can create a more balanced ecosystem that supports beneficial insects and predators, which can help control pest populations. For example, planting marigolds alongside vegetables can repel certain pests, while attracting pollinators that benefit the garden as a whole. Additionally, the diversity of plant species can help to disrupt the life cycles of pests and diseases, reducing the spread of infestations.

Intercropping also allows for better use of pollination services. This increased pollinator activity can enhance the productivity of flowering crops and contribute to higher overall yields. For instance, planting flowering herbs like lavender or cilantro near fruiting vegetables like peppers and cucumbers can attract pollinators and improve fruit set and quality.

There are several common intercropping strategies that gardeners can employ to maximize yields.

- **Strip cropping** involves growing different crops in alternating rows or strips, which can help to manage soil erosion and improve resource use.

- **Row intercropping** places different crops in separate rows within the same field, allowing for easy maintenance and harvesting while maximizing space.

- **Mixed intercropping** involves planting different crops together in the same area without distinct rows, which can enhance biodiversity and create a more complex plant environment. Each strategy has its own set of advantages and can be chosen based on the specific goals and conditions of the garden.

When planning an intercropping system, it's important to consider factors such as plant height, growth habit, and nutrient requirements. Tall plants, like corn or tomatoes, can be grown alongside shorter plants, such as lettuce or radishes, to make efficient use of vertical space. Additionally, plants with similar or complementary nutrient needs should be selected to prevent competition and ensure optimal growth.

PART 4
HARVESTING AND PRESERVATION

CHAPTER 15

HARVESTING TECHNIQUES

Harvesting techniques are a fundamental aspect of survival gardening, essential for ensuring that your crops are gathered at their peak quality and readiness. Proper harvesting not only maximizes the yield and nutritional value of your produce but also contributes to the efficiency and success of your survival garden. Each type of crop requires specific techniques and timing to achieve the best results, and mastering these can significantly enhance your ability to sustain yourself and your family.

Timing is crucial when it comes to harvesting. Different crops have varying indicators of ripeness, and understanding these signs is key to optimizing your harvest. Root vegetables like carrots, beets, and radishes should be harvested when they've reached their full size but before they become overgrown and tough. For example, carrots are typically ready when they are about 1/2 to 1 inch in diameter. Leafy greens such as spinach, kale, and lettuce can be harvested continuously by picking the outer leaves first, allowing the inner leaves to keep growing. Fruiting vegetables, including tomatoes and peppers, should be collected when they have achieved their mature color and firmness. Regular observation of your plants will help you gauge the right time to harvest and prevent overripe or underripe produce.

Different crops require specific harvesting techniques. For root vegetables, such as carrots and beets, use a garden fork or hand trowel to gently loosen the soil around the roots before lifting them out. Avoid pulling directly on the greens to prevent damaging the roots. Potatoes should be harvested after the foliage has died back, ensuring that the tubers are fully mature. Leafy greens are harvested by using clean, sharp scissors to cut the leaves from the plant, starting with the outer, older leaves and leaving the younger leaves to continue growing. Fruiting vegetables should be cut from the plant with garden shears, leaving a short stem to reduce damage. For herbs like basil, mint, and rosemary, cut the stems just above a leaf node to encourage new growth.

Best practices for harvesting include maintaining cleanliness and care. Use clean, sharp tools to prevent the spread of disease and pests. Always handle produce gently to avoid bruising or damage. For root vegetables, careful digging and lifting prevent breaking or splitting. After harvesting, proper storage is crucial to extending the shelf life of your produce. Root vegetables should be stored in a cool, dark, and dry place, while leafy greens and herbs are best kept in the refrigerator. Fruiting vegetables can be stored at room temperature until ripe, then moved to the fridge if needed. Consider preservation techniques such as canning, drying, or freezing to extend the availability of your produce. Regular harvesting promotes continued growth and productivity, ensuring a steady supply of fresh food.

In survival situations, efficient harvesting techniques become even more critical. The ability to harvest crops quickly and effectively can significantly impact your food security and overall self-sufficiency. Planning your harvest schedule to align with peak production times and prioritizing crops that are essential for immediate needs will help maximize your food supply. Developing skills in both harvesting and preservation ensures that you can make the most of your survival garden, maintaining a reliable and nutritious food source even in challenging circumstances.

WHEN AND HOW TO HARVEST

Harvesting is a crucial step in gardening that ensures you get the maximum quality and yield from your crops. The timing and method of harvesting depend on the type of plant and the specific crop. Understanding when and how to harvest each type of plant is essential for maintaining the nutritional value and flavor of your produce, as well as for maximizing your garden's productivity.

TIMING YOUR HARVEST

The timing of harvest varies widely among different types of crops. For root vegetables such as carrots, beets, and radishes, it is important to harvest them when they are mature but not overgrown. Carrots are typically ready when they reach a diameter of 1/2 to 1 inch, depending on the variety. Beets are usually harvested when they are about 1 to 2 inches in diameter. Radishes should be picked while they are still small and tender, as they can become woody if left too long. Leafy greens like spinach, kale, and lettuce can be harvested multiple times. For spinach and lettuce, harvest the outer leaves first while leaving the center to continue growing. Kale can be harvested by picking the older, larger leaves from the outside, allowing younger leaves to grow. For herbs like basil, mint, and rosemary, harvest them before they flower to ensure the best flavor. For basil, pinch off the leaves and stems just above a node. Mint can be harvested by cutting the stems, and rosemary can be trimmed back to encourage new growth.

FRUITING VEGETABLES

Fruiting vegetables, such as tomatoes, peppers, and cucumbers, have specific signs of ripeness. Tomatoes should be harvested when they have turned their mature color (red, orange, yellow, or whatever is characteristic of the variety) and are firm but slightly soft to the touch. If the tomatoes are not fully ripe when you harvest them, you can ripen them indoors. Peppers should be picked when they have reached their full color and size for the variety, and they should feel firm. Cucumbers should be harvested while they are still young and tender; if left too long, they can become bitter and overly large. To harvest, use sharp garden shears or scissors to cut the fruit from the plant, leaving a short stem attached.

ROOT AND BULB VEGETABLES

Harvesting root and bulb vegetables requires careful handling to avoid damage. Carrots, beets, and radishes should be loosened from the soil with a garden fork or hand trowel. Gently lift the roots out, taking care not to break or bruise them. For potatoes, wait until the plant's foliage has died back before harvesting. Use a fork or shovel to carefully dig up the tubers, being cautious not to puncture them. After digging, allow potatoes to cure in a cool, dark place for a couple of weeks to toughen their skins before storage.

HARVESTING FOR PRESERVATION

When planning for long-term food storage, such as canning or drying, timing is crucial. Vegetables and fruits should be harvested at their peak ripeness to ensure the best quality for preservation. For example, beans should be harvested when the pods are firm but still green if you intend to eat them fresh or when the pods are dry if you plan to save them for seeds. Fruits like apples should be picked when they are firm and have developed their full color and flavor. Once harvested, prepare them promptly for preservation to maintain their freshness and quality.

GENERAL BEST PRACTICES

- Regardless of the crop, maintaining cleanliness during harvesting is essential.

- Always use clean, sharp tools to minimize damage to the plants and reduce the risk of spreading diseases.

- Handle the produce gently to avoid bruising or breaking, which can lead to spoilage.

- For root crops, avoid pulling on the foliage, as this can break the roots. Instead, use tools to loosen the soil around the crops.

- For leafy greens and herbs, use scissors or shears to cut the leaves or stems cleanly.

POST-HARVEST HANDLING AND STORAGE

Proper post-harvest handling and storage are critical for maintaining the quality of your produce. After harvesting, clean vegetables and fruits to remove soil and debris. Store root vegetables in a cool, dark, and dry place to extend their shelf life. Leafy greens should be refrigerated and used within a week for the best freshness. Herbs can be stored in the refrigerator or dried for long-term use. Fruiting vegetables like tomatoes and peppers can be stored at room temperature until fully ripe, then moved to the refrigerator if not consumed immediately. For long-term storage, consider methods such as canning, freezing, or dehydrating.

PROPER HARVESTING TOOLS

Proper harvesting tools are essential for efficiently and effectively collecting your crops while minimizing damage to the plants and produce. Each type of crop may require specific tools designed to handle its particular needs, and using the right tools not only ensures a smooth harvesting process but also helps maintain the quality and longevity of your produce. Here's a comprehensive guide to essential harvesting tools, their uses, and how to choose and maintain them.

1. Pruning Shears

Pruning shears, also known as hand pruners or secateurs, are indispensable for harvesting many types of crops, particularly those with delicate stems or branches. They are ideal for cutting herbs, leafy greens, and small fruiting vegetables like tomatoes and peppers. Look for shears with sharp, stainless steel blades and comfortable grips. For optimal performance, choose bypass shears, which cut by bypassing one blade over another, similar to scissors, rather than anvil shears that crush the stem.

2. Garden Scissors

Garden scissors are useful for harvesting herbs, flowers, and small vegetables. They are versatile and often feature long, thin blades that can make precise cuts. Garden scissors are particularly handy for delicate tasks like snipping off basil leaves or mint stems without damaging the plant. They are also useful for trimming excess foliage and small, fragile crops.

3. Harvesting Knife

A sharp, specialized harvesting knife is useful for crops that require more substantial cutting or slicing, such as melons, squash, and large fruiting vegetables. These knives often have a curved blade that allows for easy slicing through tough skins or stems. Look for a knife with a sturdy, ergonomic handle to ensure comfortable use during extended harvesting sessions.

4. Garden Fork

Garden forks are essential for harvesting root vegetables like carrots, beets, and potatoes. They help to loosen the soil around the roots without damaging them. A garden fork typically has several strong, pointed tines that can penetrate the soil and lift out the roots with minimal disturbance. Choose a fork with a comfortable, well-balanced handle for ease of use.

5. Hand Trowel

A hand trowel is another valuable tool for harvesting root vegetables. It's particularly useful for digging around and lifting up smaller roots, such as radishes and turnips. A hand trowel should have a sturdy, sharp blade and a comfortable handle to make digging and scooping easier.

6. Harvesting Basket or Crate

A harvesting basket or crate is essential for collecting and transporting your produce. Baskets are typically lightweight and have ventilation holes to prevent produce from getting damaged or bruised. Crates are more robust and can hold larger quantities of produce. Choose baskets or crates that are easy to carry and clean, and consider using ones with handles for added convenience.

7. Garden Hoe

While primarily used for weeding and soil preparation, a garden hoe can also assist in harvesting certain crops. For example, a hoe can help loosen soil around root vegetables or cut down plants in preparation for harvesting. Choose a hoe with a sharp, strong blade and a comfortable handle.

8. Mulch and Compost Fork

A mulch and compost fork is useful for turning and distributing compost or mulch, which can help prepare soil for future planting or improve the soil's health before harvesting. While not directly used in harvesting, maintaining soil quality with this tool contributes to the overall success of your garden.

9. Harvesting Gloves

While not a cutting tool, durable harvesting gloves protect your hands from thorns, rough stems, and soil, making the harvesting process more comfortable and less prone to injury. Look for gloves made of breathable, flexible material that provides good grip and dexterity.

10. Loppers

Loppers are used for cutting larger branches and stems that may be in the way of harvesting or need to be pruned for better access. They have long handles and a sharp, powerful blade that can handle thicker branches. Loppers are particularly useful for harvesting fruit from trees or shrubs.

Choosing the Right Tools

When selecting harvesting tools, consider the following factors:

- **Quality:** Invest in high-quality tools made from durable materials. Stainless steel blades, for instance, resist rust and stay sharp longer.

- **Comfort:** Ergonomic handles and balanced designs can make the harvesting process more comfortable and reduce strain on your hands and wrists.

- **Maintenance:** Regularly clean and sharpen your tools to keep them in good working condition. Store them in a dry place to prevent rust and damage.

Maintaining Your Tools

Proper maintenance of your harvesting tools extends their lifespan and ensures they function effectively. Clean tools after each use to remove soil and plant residue. Sharpen blades regularly to maintain cutting efficiency and avoid damaging plants. Lubricate moving parts, such as the hinges on pruners or shears, to ensure smooth operation. Store tools in a dry, protected area to prevent rust and wear.

STORING FRESH PRODUCE

Storing fresh produce properly is essential for extending its shelf life, maintaining its nutritional value, and reducing food waste. Effective storage methods can help ensure that your harvest remains fresh and usable for as long as possible. Here's a comprehensive guide on how to store various types of fresh produce, focusing on best practices and techniques to keep your fruits and vegetables in optimal condition.

1 → UNDERSTANDING STORAGE NEEDS

Different types of produce have varying storage requirements based on their characteristics. Temperature, humidity, and airflow are crucial factors in maintaining freshness. Some fruits and vegetables should be stored at room temperature, while others need refrigeration or specific conditions to keep them from spoiling.

Room Temperature Storage

Certain fruits and vegetables are best kept at room temperature until they reach their full ripeness or until you are ready to use them. Tomatoes, for instance, continue to ripen at room temperature and should not be refrigerated until fully ripe, as cold temperatures can affect their flavor and texture. Similarly, bananas, avocados, and peaches should be stored at room temperature until they ripen, after which they can be moved to the fridge to prolong their freshness.

Refrigerated Storage

Many fruits and vegetables benefit from being stored in the refrigerator. Leafy greens like spinach, lettuce, and kale, as well as herbs like basil, mint, and parsley, should be kept in the refrigerator to prevent wilting and spoilage. Vegetables such as carrots, celery, and bell peppers also last longer in the fridge, where the cooler temperature slows down the aging process. Fruits like apples and berries should be refrigerated to maintain their freshness and prevent them from becoming overripe.

2 → BEST PRACTICES FOR STORAGE

1. Temperature Control

Keep your refrigerator at a consistent temperature of 35-40°F (1.6-4.4°C) to ensure optimal freshness for perishable items. Use a thermometer to monitor the temperature and adjust the settings as needed. For produce that needs to be stored at room temperature, ensure that the area is cool, dry, and away from direct sunlight.

2. Humidity Management

Humidity levels play a significant role in the storage of fresh produce. Some vegetables, such as carrots and celery, benefit from higher humidity, which can be achieved by storing them in the crisper drawers of your refrigerator, often equipped with humidity controls. On the other hand, fruits like apples release ethylene gas, which can accelerate the ripening of nearby produce. Store ethylene-producing fruits separately from other fruits and vegetables to avoid premature spoilage.

3. Airflow and Ventilation

Proper airflow helps prevent mold and rot. Store fruits and vegetables in perforated plastic bags or containers that allow for ventilation. Avoid overpacking your fridge or storage containers, as this can restrict airflow and cause produce to spoil more quickly. For root vegetables like potatoes and onions, use mesh bags or bins to allow air circulation and prevent sprouting or rotting.

4. Proper Containers

Use appropriate containers for different types of produce. For leafy greens, herbs, and berries, use breathable containers or perforated plastic bags to maintain freshness. Store root vegetables in cool, dark containers to prevent sprouting and preserve their quality. Avoid storing produce in plastic bags without ventilation, as this can trap moisture and lead to mold growth.

3 → SPECIFIC STORAGE TECHNIQUES FOR COMMON PRODUCE

1. Leafy Greens and Herbs

Leafy greens like spinach, kale, and lettuce should be washed, dried thoroughly, and stored in the refrigerator in a container lined with paper towels to absorb excess moisture. Herbs can be stored similarly or placed in a jar with a small amount of water, covered with a plastic bag, and kept in the fridge.

2. Root Vegetables

Root vegetables such as carrots, beets, and potatoes should be stored in a cool, dark place. Carrots and beets can be kept in the crisper drawer of the fridge or in a perforated plastic bag to maintain freshness. Potatoes should be stored in a well-ventilated container in a cool, dark pantry. Avoid storing potatoes with onions, as they can cause each other to spoil more quickly.

3. Fruits

Fruits like apples, pears, and berries should be stored in the refrigerator to keep them fresh. Apples and pears can be kept in the crisper drawer or in perforated plastic bags. Berries should be washed just before use to prevent excess moisture from causing mold. Bananas, avocados, and tomatoes should be kept at room temperature until they ripen and can then be moved to the refrigerator.

4. Fruiting Vegetables

Vegetables such as tomatoes, peppers, and cucumbers should be stored at room temperature until fully ripe. Once ripe, tomatoes can be refrigerated to extend their shelf life, but their flavor may be slightly affected. Peppers and cucumbers can be kept in the fridge if not used immediately.

CHAPTER   16

FOOD PRESERVATION METHODS

CANNING AND BOTTLING

Canning and bottling are essential techniques for preserving fruits, vegetables, and other produce from your garden, allowing you to enjoy your harvest long after the growing season has ended. These methods extend the shelf life of your food, making it possible to store and use seasonal produce year-round. Here's a comprehensive guide to the basics of canning and bottling, including the types of canning methods, the equipment you'll need, and best practices for ensuring food safety and quality.

Canning involves processing food in sealed jars or cans to kill microorganisms and prevent spoilage. The two primary methods of canning are water bath canning and pressure canning. Bottling, often used interchangeably with canning, typically refers to the preservation of liquids like juices, sauces, or syrups.

TYPES OF CANNING METHODS

1. Water Bath Canning

Water bath canning, also known as boiling water canning, is suitable for high-acid foods, which include fruits, fruit juices, tomatoes, jams, jellies, pickles, and some sauces. The high acidity prevents the growth of bacteria, making it safe to use this method.

Steps for Water Bath Canning:

1. Prepare Jars and Lids: Sterilize jars and lids by placing them in a pot of boiling water for 10 minutes or running them through a dishwasher cycle. Ensure lids are new or in good condition, as they are crucial for sealing.

2. Prepare Food: Wash, peel, chop, or cook your produce according to your recipe. For fruits and vegetables, follow specific recipes to ensure proper acidity and consistency.

3. Fill Jars: Pack food into jars, leaving appropriate headspace as specified in your recipe. This space is necessary for the expansion of food during processing and to ensure a proper seal.

4. Remove Air Bubbles: Use a clean knife or spatula to gently remove air bubbles by running it around the inside edge of the jar.

5. Wipe Jar Rims: Clean the rims of the jars with a damp cloth to remove any food residue that might interfere with sealing.

6. Seal Jars: Place lids on jars and screw on metal bands until they are fingertip-tight. Avoid over-tightening.

7. Process Jars: Lower the jars into a canner filled with boiling water, ensuring they are fully submerged. Process according to your recipe's recommended time, which varies by food type and altitude.

8. Cool Jars: After processing, remove jars from the canner and place them on a clean towel or cooling rack. Allow them to cool completely before storing.

2. Pressure Canning

Pressure canning is necessary for low-acid foods, such as vegetables, meats, poultry, and seafood. Unlike water bath canning, pressure canning uses steam under high pressure to reach temperatures higher than boiling water, effectively killing bacteria and other microorganisms.

Steps for Pressure Canning:

1. Prepare Jars and Lids: Sterilize jars and lids as described for water bath canning.

2. Prepare Food: Wash, cut, and cook your food according to the recipe. Pre-cooking some foods may be necessary.

3. Fill Jars: Pack food into jars, leaving the specified headspace.

4. Remove Air Bubbles and Wipe Rims: Follow the same procedure as for water bath canning.

5. Seal Jars: Apply lids and screw on metal bands.

6. Process Jars: Place jars in a preheated pressure canner. Lock the lid, and heat the canner to build pressure. Follow the recipe for processing time and pressure level, adjusting for altitude as necessary.

7. Cool Jars: After processing, let the pressure canner cool naturally. Once the pressure has returned to normal, carefully remove the jars and let them cool completely.

Equipment Needed for Canning and Bottling

1. Canner: For water bath canning, a large, deep pot with a rack is needed to hold jars and keep them off the bottom. For pressure canning, a pressure canner with a locking lid and pressure gauge is required.

2. Jar Lifters: These are specially designed tongs for safely lifting hot jars from the canner.

3. Funnel: A canning funnel helps to fill jars without spilling and ensures the correct headspace.

4. Ladle: Used to transfer food into jars.

5. Magnetic Lid Lifter: A tool for lifting sterilized lids from hot water without touching them.

6. Jar Wrench: Helps to tighten or loosen metal bands on jars.

7. Clean Cloths: For wiping jar rims and cleaning up spills.

8. Timer: To keep track of processing times accurately.

Best Practices for Safe Canning and Bottling

1. Follow Recipes: Use tested and approved recipes to ensure the correct balance of acidity and processing times. Improperly processed foods can lead to spoilage or botulism.

2. Maintain Cleanliness: Ensure all equipment, jars, and lids are properly sterilized. Work in a clean environment to minimize contamination risks.

3. Check Seals: After cooling, check that each jar has sealed properly. The lid should be concave and should not pop up when pressed. If a jar hasn't sealed, it can be refrigerated and used immediately or reprocessed.

4. Label and Date: Label jars with the contents and the date of processing. This helps track how long items have been stored and ensures you use older items first.

5. Store Properly: Store sealed jars in a cool, dark, and dry place. Avoid storing them in areas with fluctuating temperatures, such as near stoves or in direct sunlight.

6. Inspect Before Use: Before using preserved food, inspect jars for any signs of spoilage, such as bulging lids, off smells, or discoloration. Discard any questionable jars.

Troubleshooting Common Issues

1. Unsealed Jars: If jars do not seal properly, check for food residue on the rims, incorrect lid placement, or insufficient processing time. Reprocess or refrigerate the jars.

2. Soft or Mushy Food: Over-processing or using overly ripe produce can lead to a soft texture. Ensure you follow recommended processing times and use fresh produce.

3. Cloudy Liquid: In canned fruits or vegetables, cloudiness in the liquid can result from overripe fruit or excessive stirring. While this does not always indicate spoilage, it can affect quality.

DRYING AND DEHYDRATING

Drying and dehydrating are terms often used interchangeably, but they refer to different processes. Drying is the general process of removing moisture from food, which can be done through various methods. Dehydrating specifically refers to the process of using heat to evaporate moisture from food, typically with the aid of a dehydrator or oven.

METHODS OF DRYING AND DEHYDRATING

1. Air Drying

Air drying is one of the simplest and oldest methods of preserving food. It involves exposing food to air, allowing the moisture to evaporate naturally. This method works best in dry, warm climates with low humidity.

Steps for Air Drying:

1. Prepare Food: Wash, peel, and cut the food into uniform pieces. For herbs, simply harvest and clean them.

2. Arrange Food: Place food on drying racks, screens, or mesh trays. Ensure pieces are spaced apart to allow for good airflow.

3. Drying Environment: Choose a well-ventilated area with low humidity and good air circulation. A sunny spot is ideal, but ensure that food is protected from insects and dust.

4. Check for Dryness: Food is ready when it is brittle and no longer pliable. Herbs should crumble easily, and fruits and vegetables should be dry and leathery.

2. Dehydrator Drying

Food dehydrators are specialized appliances designed to remove moisture from food efficiently. They use a combination of heat and airflow to speed up the drying process and can be used for a variety of foods, including fruits, vegetables, herbs, and meats.

Steps for Using a Dehydrator:

1. Prepare Food: Wash, peel, and cut food into uniform pieces. Some foods may require blanching, especially vegetables, to preserve color and texture.

2. Arrange Food: Place food on dehydrator trays in a single layer, ensuring pieces do not overlap.

3. Set Temperature: Adjust the dehydrator to the appropriate temperature based on the type of food. Most dehydrators have specific settings for fruits, vegetables, and meats.

4. Monitor Drying: Check food periodically for doneness. Dehydrator drying times vary depending on the food and its moisture content.

5. Cool and Store: Allow dried food to cool before storing it in airtight containers.

3. Oven Drying

Oven drying is another method that can be used if you don't have a dehydrator. It involves using your oven to remove moisture from food.

Steps for Oven Drying:

1. Prepare Food: Wash, peel, and cut food into uniform pieces. Preheat the oven to the lowest setting, usually around 140-170°F (60-75°C).

2. Arrange Food: Place food on a baking sheet or oven-safe racks. Ensure that pieces are evenly spaced for uniform drying.

3. Drying Process: Leave the oven door slightly ajar to allow moisture to escape and maintain airflow. Check food frequently, turning pieces occasionally to ensure even drying.

4. Cool and Store: Once the food is dry and brittle, remove it from the oven and let it cool. Store in airtight containers.

4. Sun Drying

Sun drying is a traditional method that uses sunlight to remove moisture from food. It is best suited for hot, dry climates with low humidity.

Steps for Air Drying:

1. Prepare Food: Wash, peel, and cut food into uniform pieces. Spread the food in a single layer on drying racks or trays.

2. Exposure to Sunlight: Place trays in a sunny location with good airflow. Cover food with cheesecloth or netting to protect from insects and dust.

3. Drying Time: Sun drying can take several days depending on the temperature and humidity. Turn food occasionally to ensure even drying.

4. Cool and Store: Once the food is fully dried and brittle, bring it indoors to cool before storing in airtight containers.

Benefits of Drying and Dehydrating

1. Preservation: Drying and dehydrating significantly extend the shelf life of food, allowing you to enjoy seasonal produce throughout the year.

2. Space-Saving: Dried foods take up less space than fresh or canned goods, making them ideal for small storage areas.

3. Nutrient Retention: Proper drying methods preserve much of the nutritional value of fruits, vegetables, and herbs, including vitamins and minerals.

4. Convenience: Dried foods are lightweight and easy to store, making them convenient for use in recipes, snacks, or emergency supplies.

5. Flavor Enhancement: Drying can concentrate the flavors of fruits and herbs, adding depth to dishes and snacks.

Best Practices for Drying and Dehydrating

1. Use Fresh Produce: Start with ripe, high-quality produce. Overripe or damaged food can affect the quality and safety of the dried product.

2. Uniform Cutting: Cut food into uniform pieces to ensure even drying. This helps prevent some pieces from becoming overly dry while others remain moist.

3. Blanching Vegetables: Blanching vegetables before drying helps preserve color, texture, and nutritional value. Blanching involves briefly boiling vegetables and then plunging them into ice water.

4. Avoid Overcrowding: Whether using a dehydrator, oven, or air drying, avoid overcrowding the drying surfaces. Proper spacing allows for better airflow and even drying.

5. Check for Doneness: Ensure food is thoroughly dried to prevent spoilage. Dried fruits should be pliable but not sticky, while vegetables should be brittle and snap easily.

6. Cool Before Storing: Allow dried food to cool completely before transferring it to storage containers. This prevents condensation and potential mold growth.

7. Store in Airtight Containers: Use airtight containers or vacuum-sealed bags to store dried food. Keep them in a cool, dark place to maintain freshness.

8. Label and Date: Label containers with the contents and date of drying to keep track of storage time and ensure proper usage.

Troubleshooting Common Issues

1. Mold: Mold growth can occur if food is not fully dried or if it is stored in a humid environment. Ensure food is thoroughly dried and store in a dry, airtight container.

2. Soft or Chewy Texture: If dried food remains soft or chewy, it may not be dried enough. Return it to the dehydrator or oven for additional drying time.

3. Inconsistent Drying: Inconsistent drying can result from overcrowding or uneven heat distribution. Ensure proper spacing and rotate trays if necessary.

4. Off-Flavors: Off-flavors can result from using overripe or damaged produce. Use fresh, high-quality ingredients and follow proper drying procedures.

FREEZING AND FERMENTATION

Freezing

Freezing is a popular method of preserving food by lowering its temperature to below the freezing point, which halts the growth of microorganisms and slows down enzymatic reactions that cause spoilage. Freezing is suitable for a wide range of foods, including fruits, vegetables, herbs, and even meats.

Benefits of Freezing

1. **Nutrient Retention:** Freezing helps preserve the nutritional content of food, including vitamins and minerals, more effectively than some other preservation methods.

2. **Convenience:** Frozen foods are easy to store and can be quickly prepared for meals, offering a practical solution for busy lifestyles.

3. **Flavor Preservation:** Properly frozen foods retain their flavor, texture, and color, often better than other preservation methods.

4. **Versatility:** Freezing is suitable for a wide variety of foods, from fruits and vegetables to prepared dishes.

Best Practices for Freezing

1. **Select Fresh Produce:** Choose high-quality, ripe produce for freezing. Freshly harvested or purchased fruits and vegetables will yield the best results.

2. **Blanch Vegetables:** Blanching involves briefly boiling vegetables and then quickly cooling them in ice water. This step helps preserve color, flavor, and texture while also inactivating enzymes that can cause spoilage.

3. **Prepare Foods:** Wash, peel, and cut fruits and vegetables into uniform sizes for even freezing. For herbs, wash and chop them before freezing.

4.   Use Freezer Bags or Containers: Store food in airtight freezer bags or containers to prevent freezer burn. Removing as much air as possible from bags helps maintain food quality.

5.   Label and Date: Label each bag or container with the contents and date of freezing to keep track of storage time and ensure you use older items first.

6.   Freeze Quickly: Freeze food as quickly as possible to maintain its quality. A fast freeze helps preserve the texture and flavor of the food.

7.   Store Properly: Keep your freezer at 0°F (-18°C) or lower to ensure that food remains safely frozen.

Freezing Techniques

1.   Flash Freezing: Spread individual pieces of food on a baking sheet and freeze them until solid before transferring them to freezer bags. This technique prevents pieces from sticking together, making it easier to portion out servings.

2.   Vacuum Sealing: Using a vacuum sealer to remove air from freezer bags before sealing can help prevent freezer burn and extend the shelf life of frozen foods.

Fermentation

Fermentation is a natural preservation method that uses beneficial microorganisms, such as bacteria, yeast, or molds, to convert sugars and other carbohydrates into acids or alcohols. This process not only extends the shelf life of food but also enhances its flavor and nutritional content.

Benefits of Fermentation

1. Nutrient Enhancement: Fermentation can increase the bioavailability of certain nutrients, such as vitamins and minerals, and create beneficial probiotics that support gut health.

2. Flavor Development: The fermentation process adds complex flavors to foods, making them tangy, spicy, or umami-rich.

3. Preservation: Fermented foods have a longer shelf life due to the acidic environment created by beneficial microorganisms, which inhibits spoilage organisms.

4. Versatility: Fermentation can be applied to a wide range of foods, including vegetables, fruits, dairy, and grains.

Basic Fermentation Techniques

1. Lacto-Fermentation: This method uses lactic acid bacteria to ferment vegetables and fruits. Common examples include sauerkraut, kimchi, and pickles.

2. Alcoholic Fermentation: Yeasts are used to ferment sugars into alcohol and carbon dioxide. Examples include beer, wine, and kombucha.

3. Acetic Acid Fermentation: This process involves converting alcohol into acetic acid using acetic acid bacteria, resulting in products like vinegar.

Steps for Fermentation

1. Prepare Ingredients: Wash and cut vegetables or fruits as needed. For vegetable fermentation, you may want to add spices or flavorings, such as garlic, dill, or ginger.

2. Create a Brine: For many vegetable ferments, you'll need a saltwater brine. The salt helps inhibit undesirable microorganisms while allowing beneficial bacteria to thrive.

3. Pack Ingredients: Place your ingredients into a clean, sterilized jar or fermentation vessel. Ensure that the food is submerged under the brine to prevent exposure to air, which can lead to mold growth.

4. Seal the Container: Use a lid or fermentation weight to keep the food submerged. Some fermentations require an airlock to allow gases to escape while keeping contaminants out.

5. Ferment: Store the jar at room temperature in a dark place. The fermentation process can take anywhere from a few days to several weeks, depending on the recipe and ambient temperature.

6. Taste and Store: Check the flavor of your ferment periodically. Once it has reached the desired taste, transfer it to the refrigerator to slow down the fermentation process and preserve the flavor.

Troubleshooting Fermentation

1.   Mold: If mold forms on the surface of your ferment, remove it promptly. Ensure that the food is fully submerged in the brine and that the container is clean.

2.   Off-Smells: A strong, unpleasant odor may indicate spoilage. Properly fermented foods should have a tangy, slightly sour smell.

3.   Texture Changes: Over-fermentation can lead to overly soft or mushy textures. Monitor your ferment regularly to ensure it remains crisp and enjoyable.

In some cases, you might combine freezing and fermentation for enhanced preservation. For example, you can ferment vegetables and then freeze them for long-term storage. This combination leverages the benefits of both methods, providing a diverse range of preserved foods.

CHAPTER 17

SAVING SEEDS FOR THE FUTURE

SEED SAVING TECHNIQUES

Seed saving is an invaluable skill for anyone committed to a sustainable and self-sufficient garden, particularly in the context of survival gardening. It encompasses a range of techniques designed to preserve plant varieties from one season to the next, ensuring a reliable and diverse source of seeds for future planting. This practice not only saves money but also helps maintain genetic diversity, adapt plants to local conditions, and contribute to long-term garden sustainability.

To begin with, choosing the right plants for seed saving is crucial. Open-pollinated or heirloom varieties are preferred over hybrids because hybrids may not produce offspring true to the parent plant's characteristics—or, in many cases, they may not produce seed at all, and if they do, there's a good chance those seeds will be sterile. This means that the next generation of plants could differ significantly in terms of yield, disease resistance, or flavor.

Understanding the pollination process of your plants is another key aspect of successful seed saving. Plants can be self-pollinated, such as tomatoes and beans, or cross-pollinated, like squash and corn. For cross-pollinated plants, it's essential to take measures to prevent cross-breeding, which could result in seeds that don't represent the true characteristics of the parent plant. This can be managed through physical isolation, planting at different times, or using barriers to prevent pollinators from transferring pollen between different varieties.

When it comes to harvesting seeds, timing is everything. Seeds should be collected when they are fully mature. For fruits and vegetables, this often means waiting until they are overripe or have dried on the plant. For example, beans should be left on the plant until the pods are dry and brittle. Similarly, flower seeds should be collected after the seed heads have dried completely. Harvesting too early can result in seeds that are not fully developed and may not germinate well.

Once harvested, seeds need to be cleaned and dried properly. For wet seeds from fruits like tomatoes or cucumbers, the seeds are scooped out and allowed to ferment for a few days to remove the gelatinous coating. After fermentation, the seeds are rinsed and dried on a paper towel or mesh screen. For dry seeds, such as those from beans or grains, the seeds are removed from their pods and spread out to dry thoroughly. Proper drying is critical to prevent mold and rot during storage.

Seed cleaning involves removing any remaining debris, such as chaff or plant material. This can be done using a fine mesh sieve or a seed cleaning machine for larger quantities. Ensuring that only viable seeds are stored helps maintain seed quality and germination rates. Once cleaned, seeds should be stored in airtight containers or envelopes to protect them from moisture and pests. Labeling each container with the plant name, variety, and date of collection is essential for keeping track of your seed inventory and ensuring that you use older seeds first.

For long-term storage, seeds should be kept in a cool, dry place. Ideal storage conditions are temperatures between 32°F and 41°F (0°C and 5°C). Adding desiccants like silica gel packets to storage containers can further protect seeds from moisture. Proper storage conditions help preserve seed viability and prevent deterioration over time. Regularly checking the stored seeds for any signs of moisture or pests can also help maintain their quality.

Selecting healthy plants for seed saving is important. Avoid seeds from plants that show signs of disease or pest damage, as these issues can be transmitted to future generations. Isolating different varieties of cross-pollinated plants and rotating crops can help prevent disease buildup and ensure that saved seeds remain true to type. Maintaining detailed records of your seed saving efforts, including the source of the seeds and any special conditions or treatments, can also help improve your techniques over time.

Testing seed viability before planting is another useful practice. This can be done by placing a few seeds on a damp paper towel and keeping them in a warm place. After a week or two, check for sprouting to gauge the seeds' germination potential. If germination rates are low, consider planting new seeds or adjusting storage conditions.

STORING AND PRESERVING SEEDS

The storing process begins with proper harvesting and cleaning, but careful storage is equally important to protect seeds from factors that could compromise their longevity. After harvesting seeds, which involves collecting them at their peak maturity and ensuring they are fully dried, the next step is to store them under conditions that maintain their quality and prevent deterioration.

Seeds should be stored in airtight containers to protect them from moisture and pests. Options include glass jars, plastic containers, or vacuum-sealed bags, all of which help create a barrier against environmental factors that can affect seed viability. It is essential to ensure that the containers are completely sealed, as exposure to air and moisture can lead to mold growth and seed rot. Each container should be clearly labeled with the plant variety, date of collection, and any relevant information about the seeds. This labeling is crucial for tracking the age of the seeds and ensuring you use the oldest seeds first.

The storage environment plays a significant role in seed preservation. Seeds should be kept in a cool, dry, and dark place to maintain their dormancy and prevent premature germination. Ideal storage temperatures are between 32°F and 41°F (0°C and 5°C), which can often be achieved using a refrigerator or a dedicated seed storage unit. Keeping seeds in a dark location helps prevent light-induced germination and degradation of seed quality. Additionally, using desiccants like silica gel packets inside storage containers can help absorb any residual moisture and further protect seeds from humidity, which is a common cause of seed spoilage.

Regularly checking stored seeds for signs of moisture, mold, or pests is also important. If any issues are detected, such as mold growth or a musty odor, it's best to discard affected seeds to prevent contamination of the remaining seed stock. For long-term preservation, consider conducting periodic germination tests. Place a small number of seeds on a damp paper towel and keep them in a warm environment to check their sprouting rate. This test helps gauge seed viability and ensures that your stored seeds are still capable of germinating effectively.

In addition to these basic practices, understanding the specific needs of different seed types can enhance preservation efforts. Some seeds, such as those from legumes or grains, might have different requirements for moisture content and storage conditions compared to seeds from fruits or vegetables. Tailoring your storage methods to the specific characteristics of each seed type can help optimize their longevity and performance.

PLANNING FOR NEXT SEASON

Planning for the next gardening season is a pivotal step in ensuring that your garden thrives and yields a bountiful harvest. It begins with reflecting on the current season, analyzing what worked and what didn't, and using these insights to guide your decisions for the upcoming season.

1 → Take time to assess the performance of your crops, noting which varieties flourished and which struggled, as well as any pest or disease issues you encountered. Documenting these observations provides a solid foundation for making informed choices and adjustments for the future.

2 → Setting clear, achievable goals for the next season is crucial. Whether you aim to increase your yield, experiment with new plant varieties, or improve soil health, having well-defined goals helps focus your efforts and resources. Consider what you want to accomplish and how you can align your gardening practices with these objectives. For example, if you want to grow more vegetables, you

might plan to expand your garden space or optimize planting techniques to maximize productivity.

3 → Crop rotation is another key component of effective garden planning. Rotating crops helps prevent soil depletion and minimizes the risk of pests and diseases. Develop a crop rotation plan that aligns with your chosen varieties, ensuring that each type of plant follows a different family in successive seasons.

4 → Selecting the right crops for the next season involves understanding your garden's specific conditions and your personal preferences. Review the results from your current season to identify which crops performed well and which did not. Use this information to choose varieties that are well-suited to your soil, climate, and growing conditions. Incorporating a mix of staple crops, experimental varieties, and companion plants can enhance the overall productivity and resilience of your garden.

5 → Soil preparation is a critical aspect of planning for the next season. Test your soil to determine its nutrient content, pH level, and structure. Based on the results, amend the soil as needed with compost, organic matter, or specific fertilizers. Preparing your soil in advance ensures that it is in optimal condition by the time you start planting. Implementing practices like mulching and cover cropping during the off-season can also improve soil health and fertility.

6 → Creating a planting schedule helps manage your time and resources effectively. Determine the optimal planting dates for each crop based on your region's climate and growing season. Factor in the time required for seed starting, transplanting, and harvesting. Use a garden planner or calendar to map out your planting and harvesting timelines, ensuring that you avoid overcrowding and timing issues.

7 → If you're saving seeds from the current season, ensure they are properly cleaned, dried, and stored for future use. Review your seed inventory and order any additional seeds you may need. For plants that need to be started indoors, such as tomatoes or peppers, prepare your seed starting supplies and plan your indoor growing setup. This early preparation allows you to get a head start on the growing season and ensures that you have healthy, strong plants ready for transplanting.

8 → Assessing and updating your garden infrastructure is also important. Check for any necessary repairs or improvements to garden structures, irrigation systems, and other equipment. Consider integrating new technologies or techniques that could enhance your gardening experience, such as rainwater harvesting systems or vertical gardening solutions. Investing in these improvements ensures that your garden is well-equipped to support your goals.

9 → Anticipating and planning for potential pest and disease issues is crucial for a successful season. Based on your previous experiences, develop strategies for managing these challenges. This might involve selecting disease-resistant varieties, using integrated pest management techniques, or implementing organic treatments. Preparing for these issues in advance helps protect your plants and maintain a healthy garden.

10 ——→ Effective budgeting and resource management are essential for successful gardening. Create a budget for the upcoming season, considering expenses for seeds, soil amendments, tools, and other supplies. Look for cost-saving opportunities, such as purchasing seeds in bulk or making your own compost. Proper budgeting ensures that you can achieve your gardening goals without overspending.

PART 5
SUSTAINABLE PRACTICES AND ADVANCED TECHNIQUES

CHAPTER 18

PERMACULTURE PRINCIPLES

INTRODUCTION TO PERMACULTURE

Permaculture is a comprehensive design philosophy that seeks to create sustainable and self-sufficient systems by emulating the natural ecosystems around us. The term "permaculture" blends "permanent" and "agriculture," reflecting its goal of establishing enduring agricultural practices and cultures that work harmoniously with the environment.

. At its heart, permaculture revolves around designing systems that function in alignment with natural processes, rather than imposing human-made methods that can disrupt ecological balance. This involves observing natural patterns and integrating them into agricultural practices, such as using swales to manage water runoff or applying mulching to retain soil moisture.

A fundamental aspect of permaculture is the idea of "designing with nature."

Permaculture seeks to replicate efficient systems in human-made gardens and farms. For instance, rather than relying on chemical fertilizers and pesticides, permaculture promotes practices like composting and the use of natural predators to manage soil fertility and pest populations. This approach supports the health of the garden and minimizes the impact on the broader environment.

Permaculture emphasizes diversity and redundancy as key components of a resilient system. Combining vegetables with herbs and flowers adds multiple layers of functionality to your garden; this design reduces the risk of crop failure and enhances productivity. Diversity also includes integrating animals into the garden, which can provide additional benefits like natural pest control and manure for fertilization. The principle of "closing the loop" is also central to permaculture, advocating for the reuse and recycling of resources within the system. This means that waste products from one part of the system, such as kitchen scraps, are repurposed as compost for the garden, creating a continuous cycle of nutrients and reducing waste.

Social and ethical dimensions are integral to permaculture as well. The approach promotes fairness and equity, ensuring that the systems benefit all participants and contribute positively to the community. This might involve supporting local economies, sharing resources and knowledge, and fostering strong community bonds.

Permaculture design follows a set of guiding principles that help in creating effective and resilient systems. Key principles include observing and interacting with the environment to understand its patterns, catching and storing energy to maximize resource use, and ensuring that the system provides tangible yields. Additionally, permaculture emphasizes the importance of self-regulation and accepting feedback to continuously improve the system, using renewable resources whenever possible, and minimizing waste through recycling and efficient resource management. Designing from patterns to details, integrating elements of the system, and valuing diversity further enhance the effectiveness of permaculture practices.

DESIGNING A PERMACULTURE GARDEN

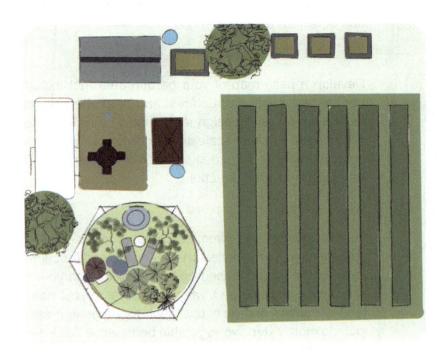

Designing a permaculture garden involves creating a sustainable and self-sufficient system that harmonizes with nature. The process begins with understanding your site's unique characteristics and then using this knowledge to develop a design that maximizes efficiency, productivity, and ecological balance. Here's a detailed guide to designing a permaculture garden, including key steps and principles to follow.

1   Site Analysis and Observation

The first step in designing a permaculture garden is conducting a thorough site analysis. This involves observing and recording various factors that will influence your garden's design. Start by assessing the topography, soil type, climate, and microclimates of your site. Identify areas that receive different amounts of sunlight, wind patterns, and water drainage. Understanding these elements will help you make informed decisions about where to place different features and plants.

Pay attention to existing natural resources and features, such as mature trees, water sources, and wildlife. These elements can be integrated into your design to enhance its functionality and sustainability. For example, placing a rain garden near a downspout can help capture and manage stormwater runoff.

2   Define Your Goals

Clarify your goals and objectives for the permaculture garden. Are you aiming to grow a diverse range of vegetables, create a habitat for wildlife, or reduce your environmental footprint? Defining your goals will guide your design decisions and help you prioritize features and functions. Consider your needs and preferences, such as whether you want a food forest, a herb garden, or a combination of various elements.

3 → Create a Base Map

Develop a base map of your garden area that includes key features such as boundaries, existing structures, and natural elements. This map serves as a foundation for your design and helps you visualize how different components will fit together. Use a scale drawing to accurately represent the dimensions and proportions of your garden space. Mark important details such as slopes, sun exposure, and wind directions.

4 → Design Zones and Sectors

Permaculture design often incorporates zones and sectors to optimize the placement of elements based on their needs and functions. Zones refer to different areas of the garden based on their proximity to your home and their intended use. For example, Zone 1, which is closest to your home, is ideal for high-maintenance plants and daily use, such as herbs and salad greens. Zone 2 might include more extensive vegetable beds, while Zone 3 could be reserved for fruit trees and larger crops. Zones 4 and 5 are typically dedicated to less intensive management, such as wild areas or forage crops.

Sectors involve analyzing external factors that influence your garden, such as prevailing winds, sun paths, and potential sources of pollution or disturbances. Design elements should be positioned to make the most of beneficial factors and mitigate negative impacts. For example, windbreaks or hedgerows can protect more delicate plants from strong winds, while sun traps can enhance solar gain for plants that need more warmth.

5 → Plan for Water Management

Water management is a critical aspect of permaculture design. Implementing strategies to capture, store, and distribute water efficiently helps create a resilient garden. Consider installing rainwater harvesting systems, such as barrels or cisterns, to collect and store rainwater for later use. Design swales or contour beds to direct and manage water runoff, preventing erosion and promoting soil infiltration.

Incorporate features like ponds or water gardens to create microclimates and support biodiversity. Drip irrigation systems can be used to provide targeted watering for plants while conserving water. Designing your garden with water management in mind ensures that your plants receive the right amount of moisture and reduces the need for additional irrigation.

6 → Choose Plants and Layout

Selecting plants that are well-suited to your climate, soil, and growing conditions is crucial for a successful permaculture garden. Choose a mix of annuals, perennials, and native species to create a diverse and resilient plant community. Consider companion planting to enhance plant health and productivity, such as pairing nitrogen-fixing legumes with heavy feeders like tomatoes.

Design your garden layout to maximize space and efficiency. Use techniques such as raised beds, vertical gardening, and interplanting to optimize growing conditions and increase yields. Create plant guilds or polycultures, where different plants support each other and contribute to the overall health of the garden.

7 → Incorporate Structures and Elements

Integrate various structures and elements into your permaculture design to enhance functionality and aesthetics. This can include garden beds, pathways, composting systems, greenhouses, and animal habitats. Use natural materials and sustainable building practices to minimize environmental impact.

Consider adding features such as trellises for climbing plants, cold frames for extending the growing season, and mulch or ground covers to suppress weeds and retain soil moisture. Structures like pergolas or arbors can provide shade and create microclimates for more delicate plants.

8 → Implement and Maintain

Once your design is complete, it's time to implement the plan. Begin by preparing the soil, installing structures, and planting according to your layout. Monitor the garden as it develops, making adjustments as needed to address any issues that arise.

Regular maintenance is key to the success of your permaculture garden. This includes tasks such as watering, mulching, pruning, and managing pests and diseases. Use organic and natural methods to maintain soil health and plant vitality. Embrace a mindset of continuous learning and improvement, adapting your practices based on observations and feedback.

9 → Evaluate and Adapt

Permaculture is an evolving process that requires ongoing evaluation and adaptation. Regularly assess the performance of your garden, noting successes and areas for improvement. Use this feedback to refine your design and practices for future seasons. Adaptation is a natural part of permaculture, allowing you to respond to changing conditions and continue enhancing the sustainability and productivity of your garden.

INTEGRATING ANIMALS INTO THE GARDEN

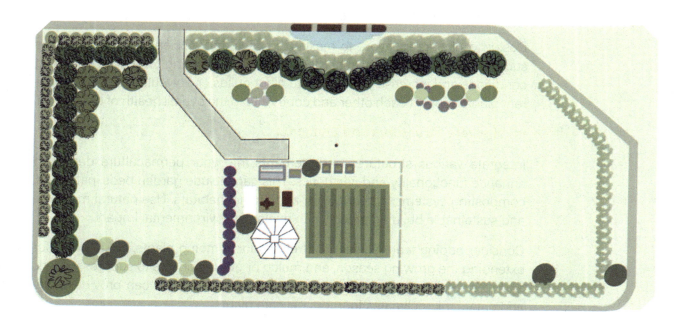

Animals play a vital role in maintaining the health and productivity of the garden by providing natural services such as pest control, fertilization, and soil aeration. When thoughtfully integrated, animals contribute to the overall resilience of the garden, enhancing its ecological functions while also offering additional resources like eggs, milk, and meat.

1 → Understanding the Role of Animals in Permaculture

In a permaculture system, animals are not just passive inhabitants; they are active participants in the ecological processes that keep the garden thriving. Each animal species brings unique benefits to the system. For instance, chickens are excellent foragers that can help manage insect populations while their droppings provide nutrient-rich fertilizer for the soil. Ducks, on the other hand, are particularly good at controlling slugs and snails, pests that can otherwise wreak havoc on your plants. Larger animals like goats or sheep can be used for grazing, which helps to control weeds and promotes healthy grass growth.

The key to integrating animals into the garden is to view them as part of a larger system where their natural behaviors and needs align with the functions they perform. This approach not only makes the garden more productive but also creates a more humane and sustainable environment for the animals themselves.

2 → Selecting the Right Animals for Your Garden

Choosing the right animals for your permaculture garden depends on several factors, including the size of your space, the resources available, and your specific goals. For smaller gardens, chickens and rabbits are often ideal choices due to their manageable size and the wide range of benefits they offer. Chickens can provide eggs and meat, and their manure is excellent for composting. Rabbits, on the other hand, produce droppings that can be used as a direct fertilizer and are also relatively low-maintenance.

If you have more space and are interested in larger livestock, consider integrating animals like goats or sheep. Goats are particularly versatile; they can clear brush, provide milk, and their droppings can be composted. Sheep are great for maintaining grassy areas and can also contribute wool if you're interested in fiber production

Aquatic systems can also be integrated into your permaculture garden, with fish or ducks playing a role in maintaining ponds or other water features. Fish can provide protein, and their waste products can be used in aquaponics systems to fertilize plants. Ducks, as mentioned earlier, are excellent for pest control and can also contribute eggs.

3 → Designing Animal Housing and Systems

Integrating animals into your garden requires careful planning of their housing and systems to ensure they contribute positively to the garden while having their needs met. Animal shelters should be designed with both functionality and comfort in mind. For example, chicken coops should be secure from predators, provide adequate space for roosting, and include nesting boxes for egg-laying. Mobile chicken coops, also known as chicken tractors, can be moved around the garden, allowing chickens to forage in different areas while spreading their manure and controlling pests.

Goat or sheep shelters should provide protection from the elements and have sufficient space for the animals to move around comfortably. Additionally, fencing should be robust enough to prevent escape while allowing the animals to graze different sections of the garden. Rotational grazing systems, where animals are moved from one paddock to another, help prevent overgrazing and promote the regeneration of plant life.

For aquatic systems, integrating a pond with fish can serve as both a water source for the garden and a habitat for the fish. The pond should be designed to maintain water quality and provide appropriate conditions for the fish species you choose. Ducks can also be housed near ponds, with access to the water to forage and swim.

4 → Integrating Animals with Plant Systems

A well-designed permaculture garden integrates animals and plants in a way that benefits both. This can be achieved through strategies like rotational grazing, where animals are moved through different areas of the garden to graze on plants or forage crops. This not only keeps the plants healthy by preventing overgrazing but also allows the animals to contribute manure to different parts of the garden, enhancing soil fertility.

Another strategy is the use of cover crops or green manures that animals can graze on. These plants are grown specifically to improve soil health and can be turned into the soil after grazing to add organic matter and nutrients. Chickens can also be allowed to forage in garden beds after the harvest season, where they will naturally scratch the soil, eat leftover seeds, and help control pests.

Aquaponics is an innovative way to integrate fish with plant systems. In an aquaponics system, fish waste provides nutrients for plants grown in water, while the plants help filter and clean the water for the fish. This closed-loop system is highly efficient and can be used to grow a variety of vegetables, herbs, and even fruits.

5 → Managing Animal Health and Welfare

Ensuring the health and welfare of animals in your permaculture garden is crucial for their productivity and the overall success of the system. Regular monitoring of the animals for signs of illness or stress is important, as is providing them with a balanced diet that meets their nutritional needs. Clean water should always be available, and their living conditions should be kept sanitary to prevent the spread of disease.

It's also important to consider the social needs of animals, particularly for species that are naturally social, like chickens or goats. Providing opportunities for social interaction and enrichment can improve their well-being and reduce stress-related behaviors.

6 → Ethical Considerations and Sustainability

Integrating animals into a permaculture garden requires thoughtful consideration of ethical and sustainability issues. This includes ensuring that animals are treated humanely and that their needs are met in a way that aligns with the principles of permaculture. This might mean choosing breeds that are well-suited to your climate and environment, reducing reliance on external inputs, and focusing on systems that allow animals to express their natural behaviors.

Sustainability is also a key concern. The goal is to create a balanced ecosystem where plants and animals support each other, contributing to the health and productivity of the entire garden.

CHAPTER 19

ADVANCED GARDENING TECHNIQUES

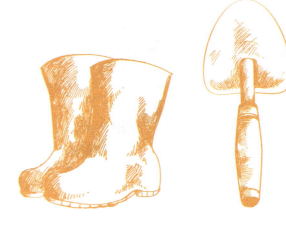

HYDROPONICS AND AQUAPONICS

Hydroponics and aquaponics are two innovative gardening techniques that have revolutionized the way we grow food, especially in urban and resource-constrained environments.

These methods offer sustainable alternatives to traditional soil-based gardening, allowing plants to thrive in controlled, soil-free systems. Hydroponics, at its core, is a method where plants are grown with their roots immersed in a nutrient-rich water solution instead of soil. This approach allows for precise control over the nutrients that plants receive, often resulting in faster growth rates and higher yields compared to conventional gardening. The nutrient solution is carefully balanced and recirculated, ensuring that plants receive an optimal mix of minerals. This not only promotes healthier plant growth but also significantly reduces water usage—by up to 90%—as the water is continuously reused within the system.

Aquaponics, on the other hand, takes the principles of hydroponics a step further by integrating fish farming with plant cultivation. In an aquaponic system, fish are raised in tanks, and their waste, rich in nutrients like ammonia, is used to fertilize the plants. Beneficial bacteria convert the ammonia into nitrates, which are then absorbed by the plants as nutrients. This creates a symbiotic relationship where the plants help filter and clean the water, which is then recirculated back to the fish tanks. The result is a self-sustaining ecosystem that produces both fresh vegetables and fish, making it a highly efficient and sustainable food production system. Aquaponics mimics natural ecosystems and requires minimal external inputs, making it an attractive option for those interested in sustainable living and reducing their environmental footprint.

Both hydroponics and aquaponics offer unique advantages, but they also come with their own set of challenges. Hydroponics is often seen as simpler and easier to manage, especially for beginners, as it requires only the maintenance of the nutrient solution and plant care. Aquaponics, while offering the additional benefit of fish production, is more complex, as it involves balancing the needs of both plants and fish, along with maintaining water quality and managing the living ecosystem. However, the rewards of aquaponics can be significant, as it not only provides a source of fresh produce but also protein, making it a comprehensive solution for food security.

Choosing between hydroponics and aquaponics depends largely on your goals, space, and level of commitment. Hydroponics is ideal for those who want to maximize plant production in small spaces, such as urban apartments or rooftops, with minimal maintenance. Aquaponics, on the other hand, is perfect for those interested in creating a more holistic, sustainable system that mimics natural processes and produces multiple types of food. Regardless of the method you choose, both hydroponics and aquaponics represent forward-thinking approaches to gardening that are increasingly relevant in today's world, where sustainable food production is more important than ever. Whether you're looking to grow fresh herbs and vegetables year-round or interested in exploring innovative agricultural techniques, these soil-free systems offer a promising path towards self-sufficiency and a more sustainable future.

URBAN AND ROOFTOP GARDENING

Urban rooftop gardening is an exciting and innovative way to transform unused or underutilized rooftop spaces into lush, productive gardens. As cities continue to grow and green spaces become increasingly scarce, rooftop gardens offer a creative solution to the challenges of urban living. They provide city dwellers with the opportunity to grow their own food, beautify their environment, and contribute to a more sustainable urban ecosystem—all while making the most of available space.

At its core, urban rooftop gardening involves cultivating plants on the roofs of buildings, whether residential, commercial, or industrial. The concept is simple but powerful: take advantage of the often-overlooked flat surfaces atop city structures and turn them into thriving green spaces. These gardens can range from small, container-based setups on apartment rooftops to large, fully landscaped green roofs that cover entire buildings. The versatility of rooftop gardening means that it can be tailored to fit a variety of spaces, budgets, and gardening goals.

One of the primary benefits of urban rooftop gardening is the ability to grow fresh, organic produce right where you live. For those living in apartments or houses with limited or no yard space, a rooftop garden can be a game-changer. Imagine stepping out onto your rooftop to harvest fresh herbs, tomatoes, lettuce, and other vegetables just a few steps from your kitchen. This not only reduces the need for trips to the grocery store but also ensures that you have access to the freshest, healthiest food possible.

Rooftop gardens also play a significant role in enhancing the aesthetics and livability of urban areas. In cities where concrete, glass, and steel dominate the landscape, adding greenery to rooftops can create a much-needed oasis of calm and beauty. Plants bring life to otherwise sterile environments, providing a welcome contrast to the urban jungle. Moreover, rooftop gardens can help improve air quality by absorbing carbon dioxide and releasing oxygen, contributing to a healthier urban atmosphere.

Beyond personal and aesthetic benefits, rooftop gardens offer a range of environmental advantages. One of the most notable is their potential to mitigate the urban heat island effect—a phenomenon where cities tend to be significantly warmer than surrounding rural areas due to the concentration of buildings, roads, and other heat-absorbing surfaces. Green roofs can help counteract this effect by providing insulation and cooling through the process of evapotranspiration, where plants release moisture into the air. This not only cools the immediate area but can also reduce the energy consumption of the building, lowering cooling costs in the summer.

Rooftop gardens also play a crucial role in managing stormwater runoff. In cities, rainwater often has nowhere to go but into storm drains, leading to increased flooding and overburdened sewage systems. Green roofs, with their layers of soil and vegetation, act as natural sponges, absorbing and retaining rainwater. This reduces the volume of runoff, decreases the risk of flooding, and helps filter out pollutants before they enter the water system. In this way, rooftop gardens contribute to more sustainable urban water management practices.

When it comes to setting up a rooftop garden, there are several factors to consider. First and foremost is the structural integrity of the roof. Not all rooftops are designed to support the weight of a garden, so it's important to consult with a structural engineer to ensure that your roof can handle the additional load. This is especially true for green roofs, which involve multiple layers, including a waterproof membrane, drainage layer, soil, and plants. Once you've determined that your roof is suitable, you can start planning the layout and design of your garden.

Container gardening is a popular and accessible option for rooftop gardens, especially for those who are new to gardening or have limited space. Containers allow you to grow a wide variety of plants in a controlled environment, and they can be moved around to take advantage of sunlight or to protect plants from harsh weather conditions. Raised beds are another option, providing a larger growing area while still being relatively easy to manage. For those with more space and resources, a full green roof—where the entire roof is covered with vegetation—can create a stunning and highly productive garden.

Selecting the right plants is key to a successful rooftop garden. Because rooftops are exposed to the elements, plants must be chosen with care, taking into account factors like sunlight, wind, and temperature fluctuations. Sun-loving plants like tomatoes, peppers, and herbs often thrive in the abundant light found on rooftops, while wind-tolerant plants such as grasses and sedums are ideal for more exposed areas. It's also important to consider the weight of the plants and soil; lighter, drought-tolerant plants are often better suited to rooftop conditions.

Watering and irrigation are critical components of rooftop gardening, as rooftop gardens tend to dry out more quickly than ground-level gardens. Drip irrigation systems, which deliver water directly to the roots of plants, can be highly effective in ensuring that your rooftop garden stays hydrated without wasting water. Additionally, installing a rainwater harvesting system can provide a sustainable source of water for your garden, reducing reliance on municipal water supplies and making your garden more environmentally friendly.

Rooftop gardening also offers opportunities for creative and innovative designs. Vertical gardening techniques, such as using trellises, wall-mounted planters, or living walls, can maximize space and create a visually striking garden. Combining different levels of planting, from low ground cover to taller plants and trees, can add depth and interest to the garden while optimizing the use of space. Incorporating seating areas, pathways, and decorative elements can turn your rooftop garden into a multifunctional space where you can relax, entertain, and enjoy the view.

Finally, rooftop gardens are not just for individual homes; they can also be a communal effort. Many urban buildings, including apartment complexes, offices, and schools, have successfully implemented rooftop gardens as community spaces. These shared gardens can bring neighbors together, provide educational opportunities, and even contribute to local food systems by producing fresh produce for residents or local markets.

INNOVATIVE GARDEN TECHNOLOGIES

Innovative garden technologies are transforming the way we approach gardening, offering new tools and techniques that make growing plants more efficient, accessible, and sustainable. From smart devices that monitor plant health to advanced systems that optimize water and nutrient use, these technologies are helping gardeners of all levels achieve better results while reducing their environmental impact. As our world becomes increasingly urbanized and resources like water and fertile land become more precious, these innovations become essential for the future of gardening and food production.

One of the most exciting developments in garden technology is the rise of smart gardening devices. These gadgets leverage the power of the Internet of Things (IoT) to bring real-time monitoring and control to your garden. For example, smart sensors can be placed in the soil to measure moisture levels, temperature, and light intensity. These sensors communicate with your smartphone or a central hub, providing you with data that helps you understand the needs of your plants. If the soil is too dry, for instance, you'll receive an alert on your phone, prompting you to water your plants. Some systems even take it a step further by automatically activating irrigation systems when moisture levels drop, ensuring that your plants are always properly hydrated without any manual effort.

Beyond soil sensors, smart watering systems have become increasingly popular among tech-savvy gardeners. These systems can be programmed to deliver the exact amount of water your plants need, based on weather conditions and soil data. This not only conserves water but also ensures that your plants get just the right amount, preventing issues like overwatering or underwatering. Some systems are even integrated with weather forecasts, automatically adjusting watering schedules based on predicted rainfall. This level of automation is particularly beneficial for busy gardeners or those who travel frequently, as it takes the guesswork out of watering and helps maintain a healthy garden even when you're not around.

Lighting technology has also seen significant advancements, particularly in the realm of indoor and urban gardening. LED grow lights, for example, have revolutionized the way we can grow plants indoors. Unlike traditional grow lights, which can be bulky and energy-intensive, LED lights are compact, energy-efficient, and customizable. They can be programmed to emit specific wavelengths of light that are ideal for different stages of plant growth, from seedling to flowering. This precision allows gardeners to create optimal growing conditions indoors, whether they're cultivating herbs on a windowsill or maintaining a full-scale indoor garden. The energy efficiency of LED lights also means they have a lower environmental impact and cost less to operate, making them a sustainable choice for indoor gardening.

Another innovative gardening technology that has gained traction is vertical gardening systems. As urban populations grow and space becomes limited, vertical gardens offer a solution by allowing plants to grow upwards rather than outwards. These systems can be as simple as wall-mounted planters or as complex as fully automated vertical farms. Vertical gardens maximize the use of space, making them ideal for small apartments, balconies, or urban rooftops. They also promote better air circulation and reduce the risk of pests and diseases, as plants are less likely to come into contact with soil-borne pathogens. Additionally, vertical gardens can be a beautiful addition to any space, serving as living art that enhances the aesthetic of your home or office.

Hydroponics and aquaponics are other groundbreaking technologies that are changing the way we think about gardening. These soil-free growing systems allow plants to thrive in nutrient-rich water solutions, making them ideal for environments where soil quality is poor or space is limited. Hydroponics, as mentioned earlier, involves growing plants with their roots suspended in water, while aquaponics integrates fish farming with plant cultivation in a symbiotic system. Both methods are highly efficient, using significantly less water than traditional gardening and producing faster growth rates and higher yields. These systems can be set up indoors or outdoors, making them versatile options for a wide range of environments.

Aeroponics is another soil-free technology that takes things a step further by growing plants in an air or mist environment. In aeroponics, plant roots are suspended in the air and periodically misted with a nutrient solution. This method allows for even greater efficiency in water and nutrient use, as the roots are exposed directly to oxygen, promoting rapid growth. Aeroponics is particularly well-suited for growing leafy greens, herbs, and other lightweight plants, and it's being used in both commercial operations and home gardens. The compact nature of aeroponic systems also makes them ideal for urban settings, where space is at a premium.

In addition to these growing systems, there have been significant advancements in gardening tools and equipment. For example, robotic lawn mowers and weeders are becoming more common, taking over time-consuming tasks and allowing gardeners to focus on more creative aspects of their gardens. These robots use sensors and GPS technology to navigate your garden, trimming grass and removing weeds with precision. They can be programmed to operate on a schedule, ensuring that your garden is always well-maintained without any manual labor.

3D printing technology has also started to make its way into the gardening world, offering new possibilities for customizing garden tools, planters, and even garden structures. With a 3D printer, gardeners can design and create their own tools, tailored specifically to their needs and the unique challenges of their gardens. This technology also allows for the creation of lightweight, durable planters that can be customized in terms of size, shape, and design. As 3D printing technology becomes more accessible, it's likely that we'll see even more innovative applications in the gardening world.

Finally, sustainable gardening practices are being supported by advancements in composting technology. Modern composters are designed to be more efficient, breaking down organic waste more quickly and with less effort. Some composters even use electricity to speed up the composting process, producing rich, fertile compost in a matter of weeks rather than months. These systems are often compact and odor-free, making them suitable for urban environments where traditional compost piles might not be practical.

CHAPTER 20

CREATING A RESILIENT HOMESTEAD

LONG-TERM FOOD STORAGE

The concept of long-term food storage has been around for centuries. Historically, people preserved food through methods like drying, smoking, salting, and fermenting to survive harsh winters, droughts, and other periods when fresh food was scarce. Today, these traditional methods are still valuable, but they are often supplemented with modern techniques and technologies that enhance the safety, shelf life, and nutritional value of stored foods.

Whether you're a seasoned prepper or someone just beginning to think about food security, understanding the principles and practices of long-term food storage can help you create a robust and resilient food supply.

One of the first steps in planning for long-term food storage is to assess your needs. Consider the number of people in your household, any dietary restrictions or preferences, and how long you want your food supply to last. A common recommendation is to aim for a minimum of three months' worth of food, though many people choose to store enough for six months, a year, or even longer. The key is to have a clear plan and to start building your supply gradually. This way, you can spread out the cost and effort, making the process more manageable.

When selecting foods for long-term storage, it's important to focus on items that have a long shelf life, are nutrient-dense, and are versatile enough to be used in a variety of meals. Staples like rice, beans, lentils, pasta, and grains are excellent choices because they are inexpensive, have a long shelf life, and provide a good base for many meals. Canned goods are another cornerstone of long-term storage. Canned vegetables, fruits, meats, and fish are preserved in a way that locks in nutrients and flavor, making them a reliable option when fresh food isn't available. However, it's essential to rotate canned goods regularly to ensure you're consuming them before they expire.

Another critical component of long-term food storage is properly packaging and storing your food to maximize its shelf life. Oxygen, moisture, light, and temperature fluctuations are the enemies of stored food, so taking steps to minimize these factors is crucial. For dry goods like grains, beans, and pasta, using airtight containers with oxygen absorbers is a common practice. Mylar bags, which are highly resistant to moisture and light, are often used in conjunction with food-grade buckets to provide an additional layer of protection. Vacuum sealing is another effective method for reducing oxygen exposure and extending shelf life.

For items like flour, sugar, and powdered milk, it's important to consider storage methods that prevent clumping and spoilage. These products should be stored in a cool, dry place, away from direct sunlight. Adding moisture absorbers or desiccants to storage containers can help keep these items dry and fresh for longer. In general, a cool, dark, and dry environment is ideal for long-term food storage. A basement or pantry that maintains a consistent temperature is often the best choice, but any space that meets these criteria can work.

Beyond dry and canned goods, there are other types of food that can be stored long-term with the right preparation. Dehydrated and freeze-dried foods are popular among preppers and outdoor enthusiasts because they are lightweight, have an extremely long shelf life, and retain most of their nutritional value. Dehydrating involves removing the moisture from food to prevent spoilage, while freeze-drying involves freezing the food and then removing the water through sublimation. Both methods significantly extend the shelf life of food, often up to 25 years or more when stored properly. These foods can be rehydrated with water when you're ready to use them, making them a convenient option for emergencies.

Fermented foods are another excellent addition to a long-term storage plan. Fermentation is a natural process that preserves food while also enhancing its nutritional value by promoting the growth of beneficial bacteria. Foods like sauerkraut, kimchi, pickles, and yogurt are not only delicious but also provide probiotics that support gut health. Fermented foods can be stored for several months, depending on the method used and the storage conditions. While they may not have the same shelf life as dried or freeze-dried foods, they offer valuable variety and health benefits.

Proper storage of fats and oils is often overlooked in long-term food storage plans, but it's crucial because these items are essential for cooking and maintaining a balanced diet. Unlike grains or canned goods, most oils have a relatively short shelf life, typically ranging from six months to a year. However, there are some strategies to extend their usability. Storing oils in a cool, dark place is essential to prevent them from going rancid. You might also consider storing solid fats like coconut oil, which has a longer shelf life than liquid oils. Alternatively, clarified butter (ghee) is shelf-stable and can last for years if stored properly.

In addition to food, it's important to store essential non-food items that support your ability to prepare and consume stored foods. This includes items like water (or a reliable water filtration system), cooking fuel (propane, wood, etc.), manual can openers, cookware, utensils, and basic hygiene products. If you rely on electricity for cooking, consider how you would prepare meals in the event of a power outage. A portable stove, solar oven, or even a simple campfire setup can be invaluable.

Long-term food storage is not just about survival—it's about ensuring comfort and nutrition during challenging times. To that end, it's important to include a variety of foods that can help prevent food fatigue. While staples like rice and beans are crucial, having a diverse selection of foods, including comfort foods and spices, can make a significant difference in maintaining morale and well-being. Consider storing items like chocolate, coffee, tea, and baking supplies, which can provide a sense of normalcy and enjoyment during difficult periods.

Rotating your food storage is a critical practice to ensure that your supply stays fresh and that nothing goes to waste. This involves regularly checking expiration dates and consuming older items first while replenishing your stock with new purchases. Some people use the "first in, first out" (FIFO) method, where the oldest items are used first, and new items are added to the back of the storage rotation. Regularly updating your inventory list can help you keep track of what you have, what needs to be used, and what needs to be replenished.

Finally, educating yourself and your family on how to use stored foods is essential. In a long-term emergency situation, you may need to prepare meals using only what you have on hand, so it's important to practice cooking with your stored foods. This not only helps you become familiar with the ingredients and techniques but also allows you to identify any gaps in your storage plan. Experiment with recipes that use your long-term storage items, and involve your family in the process so everyone feels comfortable and confident.

ENERGY AND RESOURCE MANAGEMENT

Managing energy efficiently means optimizing how you use and conserve energy resources, whether for powering garden tools, maintaining greenhouse temperatures, or running household systems. As energy costs rise and environmental concerns grow, adopting practices that reduce energy consumption and enhance efficiency becomes increasingly important.

Renewable energy sources, such as solar and wind power, offer viable solutions for reducing reliance on traditional energy grids. Solar panels can be used to power garden lighting, irrigation systems, and even small appliances, providing a clean and sustainable energy source. Similarly, wind turbines can generate electricity in areas with consistent wind, further diversifying energy options and promoting independence from conventional power sources.

In addition to renewable energy, energy-efficient technologies and practices are essential for managing energy consumption. Switching to LED lights, for example, can significantly cut energy use compared to traditional incandescent bulbs. This is particularly beneficial for indoor gardening, where LED grow lights can be tailored to specific wavelengths to enhance plant growth while using less power. Outdoor spaces can also benefit from motion-sensor lighting, which conserves energy by activating only when needed. Another critical aspect of energy management is heating and cooling. Utilizing energy-efficient appliances, proper insulation, and programmable thermostats can help regulate home temperatures and reduce energy waste, contributing to overall efficiency and lower utility bills.

Resource management, particularly concerning water and soil, is equally crucial for effective survival gardening. Water conservation is a primary concern, especially in regions prone to drought or limited water supply. Efficient irrigation systems, such as drip irrigation or soaker hoses, deliver water directly to plant roots, minimizing evaporation and runoff. This method ensures that plants receive adequate moisture while conserving water. Rainwater harvesting is another effective strategy for managing water resources. Rain barrels or cisterns can capture runoff from roofs or other surfaces, providing a sustainable and cost-effective water source for irrigation.

Soil management is integral to resource efficiency in gardening. Healthy soil supports robust plant growth and reduces the need for synthetic fertilizers and pesticides. Practices such as composting, mulching, and crop rotation contribute to soil health and fertility. Composting kitchen scraps and garden waste creates nutrient-rich organic matter that enhances soil structure and reduces the reliance on commercial fertilizers. Mulching conserves soil moisture, suppresses weeds, and improves soil quality as it decomposes. Crop rotation and polycultures further support soil fertility and reduce pest and disease issues by preventing nutrient depletion and promoting a balanced ecosystem.

Effective resource management extends beyond the garden into the home. Reducing energy consumption through efficient appliances, insulation, and smart home technologies can significantly lower your energy bills and environmental impact. Energy-efficient appliances, such as refrigerators, washing machines, and stoves, use less energy and reduce greenhouse gas emissions. Proper insulation helps maintain consistent indoor temperatures, reducing the need for excessive heating or cooling. Smart home technologies, including programmable thermostats and energy monitors, provide real-time data on energy usage and help identify opportunities for improvement.

Waste reduction and recycling are also important components of resource management. In the garden, composting plant debris and kitchen scraps creates valuable organic matter for soil enrichment. Recycling containers and opting for reusable items, such as cloth bags and durable storage solutions, helps cut down on single-use plastics and disposable products. These practices contribute to a more sustainable lifestyle and support long-term resource efficiency.

BUILDING COMMUNITY RESILIENCE

Community resilience involves more than just individual preparedness; it requires fostering strong, interconnected networks that support collective well-being and adaptability. The goal is to create communities that are not only able to withstand disruptions but also to recover and thrive in the face of adversity. This process involves enhancing local resources, strengthening social ties, and encouraging collaborative problem-solving.

One of the fundamental elements of building community resilience is enhancing local self-sufficiency. This can be achieved through initiatives such as community gardens, local food systems, and sustainable energy projects. Community gardens, for instance, provide a shared space where residents can grow their own food, fostering not only a sense of accomplishment and self-reliance but also offering a valuable resource during times of food scarcity. These gardens can serve as educational platforms for teaching sustainable farming practices, nutrition, and self-sufficiency skills.

Similarly, local food systems can enhance resilience by creating a network of producers, distributors, and consumers within a community. Farmers' markets, cooperatives, and food-sharing initiatives help strengthen local economies and reduce dependency on global supply chains. Supporting local agriculture and food processing not only ensures a more reliable food source but also contributes to the overall economic stability of the community. These systems also offer opportunities for collaboration and innovation, allowing residents to work together to address food security and sustainability challenges.

Sustainable energy projects, such as solar or wind power initiatives, also play a crucial role in community resilience. Community solar gardens, where multiple households invest in and benefit from a shared solar array, are an example of how collective efforts can lead to significant energy savings and increased sustainability. These projects not only provide a stable energy source but also create opportunities for community engagement and shared responsibility.

Strengthening social ties and networks is another key aspect of building community resilience. Strong social connections provide emotional support, facilitate resource sharing, and enhance collective problem-solving capabilities. Community events, such as neighborhood gatherings, workshops, and volunteer activities, help build trust and foster a sense of belonging among residents. These interactions create a supportive environment where people are more likely to collaborate and assist each other during times of need. Developing strong relationships within a community also helps to identify and mobilize local resources more effectively, enhancing the community's ability to respond to and recover from crises.

Encouraging collaborative problem-solving and preparedness planning is essential for building resilience. Communities that engage in proactive planning and scenario-based exercises are better equipped to handle emergencies and recover quickly. This involves identifying potential risks, developing contingency plans, and conducting regular drills to ensure readiness. Engaging a diverse group of stakeholders, including local government officials, emergency responders, businesses, and community organizations, ensures that plans are comprehensive and inclusive. Collaborative planning also helps to build a shared understanding of risks and responsibilities, creating a more coordinated and effective response during emergencies.

Education and training play a vital role in enhancing community resilience. Providing residents with knowledge and skills related to emergency preparedness, first aid, and disaster response empowers them to take action and support others in times of need. Workshops, training sessions, and informational resources can help residents understand the risks they face and the steps they can take to protect themselves and their families.

Effective communication is another crucial element of community resilience. Establishing clear channels of communication ensures that information flows smoothly during emergencies, reducing confusion and improving coordination. Communities can utilize various communication tools, including social media, community bulletin boards, and local radio stations, to disseminate information and updates. Having a communication plan in place helps to keep residents informed, address concerns, and provide guidance during crises. It also facilitates the sharing of resources and support among community members.

Building community resilience also involves fostering inclusivity and equity. Ensuring that all residents have access to resources, support, and opportunities for involvement is essential for creating a strong and cohesive community. This includes addressing the needs of vulnerable populations, such as the elderly, disabled, and low-income families, and providing targeted assistance to ensure their well-being. Inclusive practices help to create a sense of unity and ensure that resilience-building efforts are effective and equitable for everyone.

GLOSSARY OF GARDENING TERMS
COMMON TERMS AND DEFINITIONS

Aeration The process of loosening soil or introducing air to promote healthy root growth and improve drainage.

Annual A plant that completes its life cycle, from germination to the production of seeds, within one growing season, and then dies.

Aquaponics A system that combines hydroponics (growing plants in water) with aquaculture (raising fish) to create a symbiotic environment.

Biennial A plant that takes two years to complete its life cycle. In the first year, it typically grows leaves, stems, and roots, while in the second year, it produces flowers and seeds before dying.

Bolt The process by which a plant quickly goes to seed, often due to stress, causing it to stop producing leaves or flowers.

Cold Frame A structure with a transparent top that protects plants from cold weather, extending the growing season.

Companion Planting A gardening technique that involves planting different crops near each other to improve growth, repel pests, or enhance flavor.

Composting The process of recycling organic waste, such as food scraps and plant material, into nutrient-rich soil amendment through decomposition.

Cover Crop A plant grown primarily to improve soil health, prevent erosion, and suppress weeds during off-seasons when the main crops are not being cultivated.

Crop Rotation The practice of changing the types of crops grown in specific areas each season to prevent soil depletion and reduce pests and diseases.

Deadheading The practice of removing faded or dead flowers from a plant to encourage further blooming and maintain plant health.

Drip Irrigation A method of watering plants slowly and directly at the root zone through a network of tubes, which conserves water and reduces evaporation.

Fertilizer A substance added to soil to supply nutrients that are essential for plant growth. Fertilizers can be organic (compost, manure) or inorganic (synthetic chemicals).

Foliar Feeding The application of liquid fertilizers directly to plant leaves, allowing them to absorb nutrients through their foliage rather than through the soil.

Fruiting Vegetables Vegetables that produce edible fruits, such as tomatoes, peppers, and squash.

Germination The process by which a seed sprouts and begins to grow into a new plant.

Greenhouse A structure, typically made of glass or plastic, that allows plants to grow in a controlled environment by trapping sunlight and heat, often extending the growing season.

Green Manure Cover crops grown to be tilled back into the soil to improve soil fertility and structure.

Harden Off The process of gradually acclimating indoor-grown seedlings to outdoor conditions by exposing them to the sun, wind, and varying temperatures before transplanting.

Hardiness Zone A geographic zone defined by climate conditions, particularly temperature extremes, which helps gardeners understand which plants can thrive in their area.

Heirloom A plant variety that has been passed down through generations without being altered by modern breeding techniques.

Hydroponics A method of growing plants without soil, using nutrient-rich water solutions instead.

Loam Ideal garden soil that is a balanced mixture of sand, silt, and clay, providing good drainage, fertility, and water retention.

Manure Animal waste used as an organic fertilizer to add nutrients and improve soil health.

Mulching The practice of covering soil with organic or inorganic material (e.g., straw, leaves, wood chips, or plastic) to conserve moisture, suppress weeds, and improve soil health.

N-P-K The three primary nutrients found in fertilizers: Nitrogen (N), Phosphorus (P), and Potassium (K), each essential for plant growth.

Organic Gardening Gardening that avoids the use of synthetic fertilizers, pesticides, or herbicides, relying instead on natural processes and organic amendments like compost and manure.

Perennial A plant that lives for more than two years, often flowering and producing seeds annually after reaching maturity.

Perlite A lightweight volcanic rock used to improve soil aeration and drainage.

Pest Any insect, animal, or organism that damages plants or disrupts their growth.

Photosynthesis The process by which plants use sunlight to convert water and carbon dioxide into food (glucose) and oxygen, fueling their growth.

Polyculture The practice of growing multiple types of plants together in the same space to mimic natural ecosystems, improve biodiversity, and reduce the risk of pests.

Pruning The practice of trimming or cutting back parts of a plant to remove dead or diseased material, improve shape, and encourage new growth.

Raised Beds A gardening technique where soil is placed in elevated garden beds, often framed with wood, stone, or other materials, allowing for better drainage and soil control.

Seedling A young plant that has just sprouted from a seed.

Soaker Hose A hose with tiny holes that slowly releases water along its length, allowing for deep and even watering of plants.

Soil Amendment A material, such as compost or peat moss, added to soil to improve its texture, fertility, or structure.

Sucker A shoot that grows from the base of a plant or from the roots, often taking away energy from the main plant.

Transplanting The process of moving a seedling or young plant from one location to another, often from a seed tray to a garden bed.

Trellis A framework or structure used to support climbing plants or vines, helping them grow vertically.

Vermiculite A mineral used in soil mixes to retain moisture and improve soil aeration.

Vermiculture The process of using worms to break down organic waste into nutrient-rich compost.

Water Table   The level below the earth's surface where the ground is saturated with water. Understanding the water table is important when planning irrigation.

Weed   Any plant growing in an unwanted location, typically competing with cultivated plants for resources.

Windbreak   A line of trees, shrubs, or other barriers planted to protect crops from strong winds, reduce soil erosion, and retain moisture.

Worm Castings   The waste produced by earthworms, which is highly nutritious for plants and can improve soil health.

Xeriscaping   A landscaping method designed to conserve water by using drought-tolerant plants, mulch, and efficient irrigation techniques.

Zoning   Refers to the practice of grouping plants with similar water, sunlight, and soil requirements in the same area of the garden.

INDEX OF PLANTS AND TECHNIQUES

A

Almond trees, *97*
Apple, *73, 94, 95, 96, 97, 152, 156, 157*
Aquaponics, *183, 186, 191*
Arbors, *141, 181*
Asparagus, *19, 23, 73*

B

Basil, *34, 73, 74, 77, 104, 105, 107, 113, 114, 117, 122, 151, 154, 156*
Basins, *49, 51*
Beans, *17, 18, 19, 21, 26, 27, 31, 32, 65, 67, 72, 74, 75, 76, 78, 117, 118, 120, 125, 126, 136, 141, 145, 146, 148, 152, 171, 194, 195*
Beets, *19, 71, 72, 76, 87, 88, 89, 122, 147, 150, 151, 152, 154, 157*
Berms, *19, 23, 49*
Berries, *18, 100, 103, 156, 157*
Berry bushes, *19, 21, 23, 26, 100, 101, 102, 103, 136*
Blackberries, *101, 102, 103*
Blueberries, *73, 101, 102, 103*
Bokashi, *46, 47*
Borage, *75*
Bottling, *158, 160, 161*
Brassicas, *76, 120, 122*
Broccoli, *73, 76, 117, 121, 122*
Brussels sprouts, *73*
Buckwheat, *76*

C

Cabbage, *73, 76, 117, 121, 122, 123*
Cacti, *60*
Calendula, *73, 111*
Canning, *14, 17, 19, 24, 27, 92, 103, 151, 152, 153, 158, 159, 160, 161*
Carrots, *18, 19, 71, 72, 75, 76, 78, 87, 88, 89, 145, 147, 150, 151, 152, 154, 156, 157*
Chamomile, *110, 111*

Cherry, *73, 91*
Chives, *113*
Cilantro, *113, 148*
Citrus trees, *95*
Cloches, *29*
Closed-loop system, *21, 184*
Clover, *44, 76, 134, 138*
Coffee, *46, 195*
Cold frames, *30, 68, 69, 83, 138, 181*
Comfrey, *75*
Companion planting, *75, 74, 78, 108, 112, 114, 122, 145, 181*
Compost tea, *47, 128*
Composting, *14, 15, 17, 18, 20, 21, 23, 28, 36, 44, 45, 46, 47, 126, 129, 178, 181, 183, 192, 196, 197, 199, 207*
Container gardening, *26, 62, 63, 64, 78, 189*
Container planting, *27, 85*
Corn, *27, 31, 72, 74, 75, 78, 133, 145, 147, 148, 171*
Cover cropping, *23, 174*
Cover crops, *36, 39, 44, 76, 134, 138, 184, 200*
Crop rotation, *23, 24, 31, 34, 36, 38, 44, 45, 75, 76, 119, 121, 122, 125, 126, 134, 139, 146, 174, 196, 200*
Cucumbers, *14, 32, 65, 67, 87, 117, 119, 120, 136, 141, 146, 148, 152, 157, 171*

D

Dandelions, *75, 134*
Deep watering, *49, 51, 96, 99*
Dehydrating, *90, 123, 153, 162, 164, 165, 194*
Desalination, *60*
Drip irrigation, *17, 19, 23, 27, 28, 29, 32, 48, 50, 51, 52, 54, 59, 113, 127, 180, 190, 196, 200*
Drying, *17, 19, 24, 27, 82, 84, 92, 151, 152, 162, 163, 164, 165, 171, 193, 194*

E

Echinacea, *73, 108, 109, 108*
Espalier, *136, 137, 143*

F

Fermenting, *24, 193*
Fertilizing, *85, 96, 99, 102, 113, 114, 138*
Four-year rotation cycle, *76*
Fruit trees, *19, 21, 23, 26, 27, 28, 33, 73, 94, 95, 96, 136, 137, 138, 143, 180*
Furrow irrigation, *52*

G

Garden beds, *28, 47, 51, 59, 62, 64, 73, 84, 85, 107, 127, 138, 146, 181, 184, 201*
Garden trowel, *42*
Garlic, *19, 72, 75, 124, 147, 168*
Grapevines, *101, 102, 136*
Gravity-fed irrigation, *54*
Green manures, *36, 44, 184*
Green walls, *142, 146*
Greenhouse, *20, 21, 24, 30, 68, 69, 181, 196, 197, 200*
Greywater, *59, 60*

H

Hand watering, *55*
Hazelnut trees, *98*
Herbs, *19, 20, 21, 22, 23, 27, 28, 32, 33, 48, 53, 65, 73, 75, 77, 104, 107, 108, 112, 113, 114, 117, 142, 143, 144, 145, 146, 147, 148, 151, 152, 153, 154, 156, 157, 162, 163, 164, 166, 178, 180, 184, 187, 188, 189, 191, 192*
Hoeing, *134*
Hydroponics, *144, 186, 187, 191, 199, 200*
Hydrozoning, *49, 59*

I

Intensive row planting, *146*
Intercropping, *145, 147, 148*
Interplanting, *145, 181*
Irrigation, *17, 19, 23, 27, 28, 29, 32, 36, 48, 50, 51, 52, 53, 54, 55, 56, 59, 60, 113, 127, 131, 133, 138, 174, 180, 190, 196, 200, 202, 207*

J

Jerusalem artichokes, *73*

K

Kale, *72, 76, 81, 89, 90, 117, 121, 15p, 152, 156, 157*
Kiwis, *141*

L

Lattice, *32, 66*
Lavender, *109, 112, 114, 148*
Leafy greens, *18, 19, 21, 26, 28, 32, 65, 72, 74, 76, 88, 89, 117, 118, 121, 150, 151, 152, 153, 154, 156, 157, 192*

Legumes,*18, 19, 72, 74, 75, 76, 147, 148, 173, 181*
Lettuce, *14, 34, 69, 75, 76, 78, 86, 89, 90, 120, 125, 126, 142, 145, 146, 147, 148, 150, 152, 156, 157, 188*
Living walls, *142, 146, 190*

M

Maize, *78*
Marigolds, *19, 34, 74, 77, 122, 145, 148*
Mint, *77, 104, 106, 107, 108, 113, 151, 152, 154, 156*
Mulch, 28, 29, 37, 38, 39, 43, 47, 51, 52, 59, 85, 88, 96, 98, 109, 125, 127, 131, 132, 133, 134, 155, 181, 202
Mulched basin, *51, 52*
Mulching, 17, 23, 27, 29, 36, 49, 52, 59, 60, 63, *87, 88, 125, 127, 130, 131, 132, 133, 134, 138, 174, 177, 181, 196, 200*
Multi-layered planting, *147*

N

Nut trees, *94, 97, 98, 99, 100*

O

Oats, *72*
Okra, *81*
Ollas, *53*
Onions, *19, 72, 75, 147, 157*
Overhead sprinklers, *44*

P

Parsley, *113, 156*
Parsnips, *78*
Pear, *95, 97, 157*
Peas, *18, 32, 65, 72, 76, 81, 146, 148*
Pecans, *98*
Peppermint, *110*
Peppers, *65, 67, 76, 86, 91, 92, 117, 119, 124, 133, 138, 147, 148, 151, 152, 153, 154, 156, 157, 174, 189, 200*
Perennial plants, *19, 21, 23, 28, 133*
Pergolas, *141, 181*
Permaculture, *177, 178, 179, 180, 181, 182, 183, 184*
Potatoes, *17, 18, 19, 26, 71, 76, 87, 88, 89, 119, 120, 121, 151, 152, 154, 157*
Pressure canning, *158, 160*
Pruning, *92, 96, 99, 102, 112, 114, 126, 135, 136, 137, 154, 181, 201*
Pumpkins, *72, 75, 119*

R

Radishes, *121, 145, 146, 147, 148, 150, 152, 154*
Rain barrels, *19, 27, 28, 49, 58, 196*
Rainwater harvesting, *14, 17, 23, 49, 54, 56, 57, 174, 180, 190, 196*

Raised bed, *18, 20, 21, 27, 29, 31, 32, 34, 44, 62, 63, 64, 65, 113, 139, 146, 181, 189, 201*
Raised bed gardening, *146*
Raspberries, *73, 101, 102, 103*
Rhubarb, *73*
Rooftop gardening, *188, 189*
Rosemary, *19, 73, 104, 107, 113, 114, 151, 152*
Row covers, *29, 30, 117, 119, 121, 122, 123, 138*
Row planting, *18, 146*
Rye, *44, 134, 138*

S

Saving seeds, *23, 170, 174*
Seed saving, *23, 82, 170, 171*
Soaker hoses, *48, 51, 54, 59, 127, 196*
Soil probe, *42*
Solarization, *121, 125, 128*
Spinach, *18, 19, 69, 72, 75, 76, 78, 86, 89, 90, 122, 146, 150, 152, 156, 157*
Square foot gardening, *18, 23, 27, 34, 145*
Squash, *17, 19, 32, 72, 74, 75, 78, 91, 92, 93, 117, 119, 123, 133, 138, 154, 171, 200*
Stacked planters, *27*
Staking, *91, 92, 136*
Strawberries, *20, 32, 118, 142*
Subsurface irrigation, *54*
Succession planting, *34, 79, 146*
Succulents, *60, 142, 144*
Sunflowers, *75*
Swales, *19, 23, 177, 180*
Sweet potatoes, *19, 71*

T

Thyme, *19, 73, 112, 113*
Tiered planting, *147*
Tilling, *36*
Tomatoes, *14, 18, 19, 21, 27, 32, 33, 34, 65, 67, 74, 75, 76, 78, 81, 86, 87, 91, 92, 108, 114, 117, 118, 119, 120, 121, 122, 124, 125, 126, 133, 136, 137, 138, 141, 145, 146, 147, 148, 151, 152, 153, 154, 155, 156, 157, 158, 159, 171, 174, 181, 188, 200*
Traditional row gardens, *30, 31*
Training, *135, 136, 137, 198*
Trap crops, *121, 24*
Trellises, *20, 27, 32, 33, 65, 66, 67, 75, 92, 135, 138, 139, 141, 143, 146, 181, 190*

V

Vermicomposting, *46*
Vertical gardening, *20, 23, 27, 78, 136, 140, 141, 146, 174, 181, 190, 191*
Vertical gardens, *32, 142, 146, 191*
Vertical hydroponic systems, *144*
Vertical planters, *142, 146*
Vining squash, *32*

W

Wall-mounted planters, *20, 32, 190, 191*
Walnuts, *98, 99*
Water bath canning, *158, 159, 160*
Water conservation techniques, *19, 27, 29, 58*
Water recycling, *60*
Watering, *28, 30, 32, 36, 37, 48, 49, 50, 51, 53, 55, 58, 59, 64, 83, 85, 87, 88, 89, 90, 92, 93, 96, 99, 102, 105, 106, 107, 109, 111, 112, 113, 114, 117, 120, 121, 122, 123, 125, 126, 127, 131, 138, 180, 181, 190, 191, 200, 201*
Weeding, *21, 30, 75, 134, 146, 155*
Wheat, *72*
Wicking beds, *52, 53*
Windbreaks, *28, 29, 180*
Winter squash, *19, 72, 92, 93*
Wire frames, *32*

X

Xeriscaping, *60, 202*

Z

Zinnias, *75*

CONCLUSION

As we wrap up our exploration of survival gardening, it's clear that both individual and collective efforts are important for creating self-sufficiency and adaptability in the face of life's uncertainties. Survival gardening, with its emphasis on growing your own food and managing resources efficiently, empowers individuals to take control of their food security and sustainability. Learning to master techniques like composting, efficient irrigation, and organic pest control, gives you an opportunity to create a thriving garden that supports your personal well-being and reduces dependency on external systems.

However, the benefits of survival gardening goes beyond the individual. When we consider the broader community context, the principles of resilience and self-sufficiency become even more significant. Building community resilience involves strengthening local networks, enhancing self-sufficiency through initiatives like community gardens and local food systems, and fostering strong social connections. These efforts help communities become more adaptable, collaborative, and capable of weathering challenges together.

Integrating renewable energy sources, improving resource management, and focusing on sustainable practices are essential components of a resilient lifestyle. Renewable resources like solar panels, efficient water use, or waste reduction, contribute to a more sustainable future and reduce our reliance on external resources. Similarly, understanding and implementing strategies for effective resource management, including energy conservation and waste reduction, support a balanced and sustainable way of life.

Ultimately, survival gardening and community resilience are interconnected. The skills and knowledge gained from gardening—such as understanding soil health, planting techniques, and harvesting methods—provide a foundation for greater self-reliance. At the same time, building a resilient community creates a supportive environment where individuals can thrive and work together to address common challenges.

In conclusion, embracing the principles of survival gardening and community resilience not only enhances personal self-sufficiency but also contributes to a more sustainable and interconnected world. As we navigate the complexities of modern life, these practices offer a path towards greater independence, collaboration, and preparedness.

Made in the USA
Columbia, SC
11 May 2025

57774690R00115